ROMAN LAW IN
EUROPEAN HISTORY

This is a short and succinct summary of the unique position of Roman law in European culture by a leading legal historian. Peter Stein's masterly study assesses the impact of Roman law in the ancient world and its continued unifying influence throughout medieval and modern Europe. *Roman Law in European History* is unparalleled in range, lucidity and authority, and should prove of enormous utility for teachers and students (at all levels) of legal history, comparative law and European Studies. Award-winning on its appearance in German translation, this English rendition of a magisterial work of interpretive synthesis is an invaluable contribution to the understanding of perhaps the most important European legal tradition of all.

PETER STEIN is Emeritus Regius Professor of Civil Law in the University of Cambridge. His many publications include *Regulae iuris: From Juristic Rules to Legal Maxims* (1966), *Legal Evolution* (1980) and *Legal Institutions* (1984).

ROMAN LAW IN EUROPEAN HISTORY

PETER STEIN

CAMBRIDGE
UNIVERSITY PRESS

CAMBRIDGE UNIVERSITY PRESS
Cambridge, New York, Melbourne, Madrid, Cape Town, Singapore, São Paulo, Delhi

Cambridge University Press
The Edinburgh Building, Cambridge CB2 8RU, United Kingdom

Published in the United States of America by Cambridge University Press, New York

www.cambridge.org
Information on this title: www.cambridge.org/9780521643795

First published 1999
Thirteenth printing 2009

Originally published in German as *Römisches Recht und Europa*
by Fischer Taschenbuch Verlag GmbH 1996
and © Fischer Taschenbuch Verlag GmbH, Frankfurt am Main
First published in English by Cambridge University Press 1999 as
Roman Law in European History
English version © Cambridge University Press 1999

Printed in the United Kingdom at the University Press, Cambridge

A catalogue record for this publication is available from the British Library

Library of Congress Cataloguing in Publication data

Stein, Peter, 1926–
Roman law in European history / Peter Stein.
p.   cm.
ISBN 0 521 64372 4 (hbk).– ISBN 0 521 64379 1 (pbk)
1. Roman law – History. 2. Law – Europe – Roman influences.
I. Title.
KJA147.S744   1999
340.5'4 – dc21   98-39112   CIP

ISBN-13 978-0-521-64379-5 paperback

Contents

Abbreviations

C.	Code of Justinian
Character	P. Stein, *The Character and Influence of the Roman civil law: historical essays*, London 1988
C.Th.	Theodosian Code
D.	Digest of Justinian
Inst.	Institutes of Justinian
TvR	*Tijdschrift voor Rechtsgeschiedenis*
ZSS (RA)	*Zeitschrift der Savigny-Stiftung für Rechtsgeschichte (Romanistische Abteilung)*

Chronology

BC	753	Foundation of Rome
	509	Constitution of the Roman republic
	450	Twelve Tables enacted
	367	Establishment of praetorship
	44	Assassination of Julius Caesar
AD	14	Death of Augustus
	c. 161	Institutes of Gaius
	212	*Constitutio Antoniniana*
	312	Conversion of Constantine to Christianity
	395	Division of the empire into east and west
	438	Theodosian Code
	476	End of western empire
	506	Visigothic Roman Law
	527–65	Reign of Justinian
	800	Coronation of Charlemagne
	c. 1140	*Decretum* of Gratian
	c. 1230	*Glossa ordinaria* of Accursius
	1256–65	*Siete partidas*
	1313–57	Bartolus
	1495	Imperial Court established
	1527–91	H. Donellus
	1588–1657	A. Vinnius
	1625	*De iure belli ac pacis* of Grotius
	1646–1716	G. W. Leibniz
	1673	*De officio hominis et civis* of Pufendorf
	1690	*Les lois civiles dans leur ordre naturel* of Domat
	1699–1772	R. J. Pothier
	1779–1861	F. K. von Savigny
	1794	Prussian *Allgemeines Landrecht*
	1804	French Code civil

1812	Austrian *Allgemeines Bürgerliches Gesetzbuch*
1817–92	B. Windscheid
1818–92	R. von Jhering
1822–88	Sir Henry Maine
1900	German *Bürgerliches Gesetzbuch*

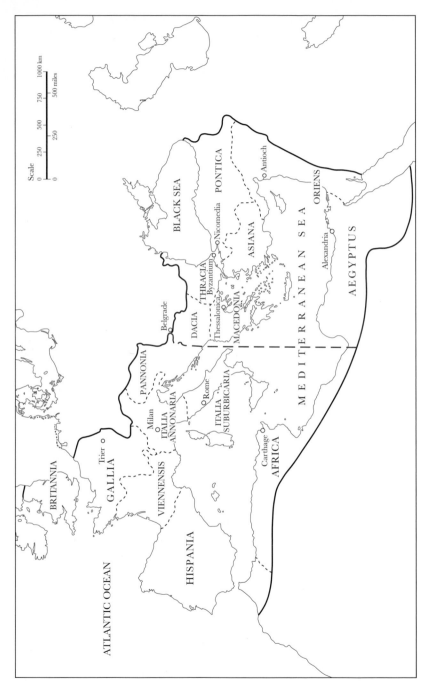

The administrative dioceses of the later Roman empire.

CHAPTER I

Introduction

When we think of the legacy of classical antiquity, we think first of Greek art, Greek drama and Greek philosophy; when we turn to what we owe to Rome, what come to mind are probably Roman roads and Roman law. The Greeks speculated a great deal about the nature of law and about its place in society but the actual laws of the various Greek states were not highly developed in the sense that there was little science of law. The Romans, on the other hand, did not give much attention to the theory of law; their philosophy of law was largely borrowed from the Greeks. What interested them were the rules governing an individual's property and what he could make another person do for him by legal proceedings. Indeed the detailed rules of Roman law were developed by professional jurists and became highly sophisticated. The very technical superiority of its reasoning, which has made it so attractive to professional lawyers through the ages, has meant that Roman law is not readily accessible to the layman. Inevitably its merits have a less obvious appeal than art or roads. Yet over the centuries it has played an important role in the creation of the idea of a common European culture.

Most of what we know about ancient Roman law derives from a compilation of legal materials made in the sixth century AD on the orders of the Byzantine Emperor Justinian. The texts that he included in this collection were the product of a thousand years of unbroken legal development, during which the law acquired certain features that permanently stamped it with a certain character. During this millennium, roughly from 500 BC to 550 AD, Rome expanded from a small city-state to a world empire. Politically it changed, first from a monarchy to a republic and then, not long before the beginning of the Christian era, to an empire. At the same time its law was adapted to cope with the changing social situation, but all the time the idea was maintained that it was in essentials the same law which had been part of the early Roman way of life.

Justinian's texts have been viewed from different perspectives by

different peoples at different periods in European history. The revival of
Roman law started in Italy, which remained the focus of its study and
development through the later middle ages. In the sixteenth century,
with the advent of humanism, France took over the leading role. In the
seventeenth century, it was the turn of the Netherlands to give a new
vision to the discipline and in the nineteenth century German scholarship transformed the subject yet again. In each period different aspects
were emphasised.

Roman law has had passionate adherents and fierce opponents. As
H. F. Jolowicz pointed out in 1947, the latter based their opposition on
three main grounds. First, it has been seen as a foreign system, the
product of an ancient slave-holding society and alien to later social ideas.
Secondly, it has been portrayed as favouring absolutist rulers and as
hostile to free political institutions. Thirdly, it has been regarded as the
bulwark of individualist capitalism, favouring selfishness against the
public good ('Political Implications of Roman Law', *Tulane Law Review*,
22 (1947), 62). Sometimes these notions have been combined. The original programme of the Nazi party in Germany demanded that 'Roman
law, which serves the materialist world order, should be replaced by a
German common law.' That attitude provoked the great German legal
historian Paul Koschaker to warn of the crisis of Roman law and to
write *Europa und das römische Recht*, eventually published in 1947.

Fifty years later a certain crisis still affects specialist Romanists but the
contribution of Roman law to European culture can be reviewed more
calmly. This book does not purport to rival that of Koschaker. It
attempts to give an idea of the character of ancient Roman law and to
trace the way its texts have constituted a kind of legal supermarket, in
which lawyers of different periods have found what they needed at the
time. It has indelibly impressed its character on European legal and
political thought. How that happened is our theme.

CHAPTER 2

Roman law in antiquity

I THE LAW OF THE TWELVE TABLES

When recorded history begins, Rome was a monarchy, but at the end of the sixth century BC the kings were expelled and a republic was established in their place. At this time, Rome was a small community on the left bank of the river Tiber not far from its estuary. Its people believed that they were descended from refugees from the city of Troy after its sack by the Greeks. Their law was a set of unwritten customs, passed on orally from one generation to the next, which were regarded as part of their folk heritage as Romans. These laws were applicable only to those who could claim to be Roman citizens (*ius civile*, law for *cives*, citizens).

In cases where the application of a customary rule to a particular case was doubtful, the interpretation of the college of pontiffs, a body of aristocrats responsible for maintaining the state religious cults, was decisive. The citizen body was divided into two social groups, the patricians, a relatively small group of propertied families of noble birth, and the plebeians, numerically larger but disadvantaged in various ways. The pontiffs were exclusively patrician and the plebeians naturally suspected that their pronouncements on the validity of particular acts and forms were not always entirely disinterested. The plebeians argued that if the customary law were written down in advance of cases arising, it would be to their advantage. They would then know what their legal position was, without having to consult the pontiffs, whose powers of interpretation would be limited to the text of the laws.

The result of this agitation was the appointment, in 451 BC, of a commission of ten citizens, the decemvirs, charged with the task of preparing a written text of the customary law, on the lines of the famous Athenian laws of Solon. They produced a collection of rules, known as the Twelve Tables, which was formally proposed to the popular assembly of citizens and approved by them. In giving its approval, the assembly did not feel that it was making new law to replace old law; rather it was fixing more precisely what had always, in general terms, been the law (*ius*). By being enacted in a text, it became *lex* (from *legere*, to read out), the public and authoritative declaration of what was *ius*.

The Twelve Tables mark the beginning of Roman law, as we know it, and its provisions ranged over the whole field of law, including public law and sacral law. The original text has not survived but there were so many quotations in later writings that its contents have been substantially reconstructed. The original order in which these fragments appeared is not clear and the versions of nineteenth-century scholars, which are printed in modern collections, certainly exaggerate the systematic character of the legislation. We do know that it began with the summons of a defendant to begin a legal action and ended with execution of the judgment at the end of an action.

The Twelve Tables did not state what everyone knew and accepted as law but rather concentrated on points that had given or might give rise to disputes. The substance of its rules was not particularly favourable to the plebeians, but the very fact that so much of the law had been put into fixed form meant that now they knew where they stood. In particular the Twelve Tables dealt with the details of legal procedure, what the citizen could do to help himself without invoking a court and what he had to do to start court proceedings. In the early republic there were few state officials to help an aggrieved person get redress for injuries which he claimed to have suffered and he had to do a lot for himself to activate the legal machinery. In certain cases self-help was tolerated, since the community was not yet strong enough to eliminate it. The Twelve Tables show, however, a determination to institutionalise such cases and keep them within strict limits.

When a dispute arose that the parties were unable to settle for themselves, they had normally to appear before a magistrate. The purpose of the meeting was to decide whether the dispute raised an issue which the civil law recognised and, if so, how it should be decided. In very early times, before the foundation of the republic, it is likely that the Romans had recourse to ordeals or oath-taking as a means of settling disputes. In the republic, however, the normal way of deciding any issue under the civil law was to refer it to a private citizen (or sometimes a group of private citizens), chosen by the parties and the magistrate. This single juryman, called the *iudex*, would investigate the facts (perhaps at first relying on his own knowledge), hear the evidence of witnesses and the arguments of the parties and deliver judgment condemning or absolving the defendant.

The problem for someone who wanted to bring such proceedings was to ensure that his opponent would attend before the magistrate for the first stage of the proceedings. The defendant might cooperate, in order to get the dispute settled, but if he did not come voluntarily, the plaintiff could force him to appear. The precise limits of this power of compulsion were not fixed by the customary law and so the Twelve Tables set out in detail exactly what the plaintiff was entitled to do. If, and only if, the defendant refused, in front of witnesses, the plaintiff's request to come to the magistrate, or tried to run away, the plaintiff could use force to compel his attendance. If the defendant was sick or aged, the plaintiff could not make him come without providing him with a conveyance of some kind, but, the law provided, it did not have to be a cushioned litter. There were certain things a man could do without going first to a magistrate. The Twelve Tables provided that, when a householder caught a thief in the act of stealing at night, or even by day if the thief resisted arrest, he could kill the thief without more ado. In most cases, however, a court ruling was necessary before direct action was allowed. In cases of serious physical injury, the parties were encouraged to reach agreement on the appropriate money payment to be made by the offender to his victim. Failing such agreement, the Twelve Tables authorised talion, that is, the victim could inflict retaliation in kind, but limited to the amount of the injury received ('an eye for an eye'). The possibility of such retaliation would act as a spur to the parties to reach agreement and talion would probably have been exercised only in cases where the offender's family could not or would not help him to find appropriate money payments. For less serious injuries no retaliation was allowed and fixed amounts of compensation were prescribed.

So far we have been concerned with disputes between individuals, but in reality a person in early Rome was more likely to be considered as a member of a group. The unit with which early Roman law was concerned was the family. The law did not deal with what went on within the family. The relations between the members was a private matter which the community had no power to control. So far as those outside the family were concerned, the family was represented by its head, the paterfamilias, and all the family property was concentrated in him. All his descendants in the male line (agnates) were in his power. A child did not cease to be in his father's power merely by becoming an adult. Until his father died, he could not own property of his own. Consequently all the family property was kept together and the resources of the family as a whole were strengthened. In practice, therefore, a claim by a victim of theft or personal injury committed by a slave or a child in power had to be brought against the family head, since he alone was in a position to satisfy that claim out of the family funds. The Twelve Tables gave him an option of either paying damages or of surrendering the delinquent into the power of the victim or of his family head (noxal surrender).

In cases of homicide there was no civil law action; rather a magistrate took the initiative on behalf of the community as a whole to prosecute the offender, thus avoiding the rise of family vendettas and blood-feuds. Normally, however, the law provided a framework within which the parties were left to settle their differences.

At the time of the Twelve Tables a plaintiff who did not receive payment of what the *iudex* had awarded him within thirty days could put pressure on the defendant up to the point of death. The plaintiff could bring him forcibly before the magistrate (there was no need for a polite request this time) and if he neither paid up nor provided a surety of substance, who would guarantee payment on his behalf, the magistrate would authorise the plaintiff to keep him in chains for sixty days. During this period he had to produce the defendant in the market place on three successive market days, to give publicity to his plight and provide an opportunity for his family and friends to deal with the matter. The ultimate threat, if this procedure failed, was the sale of the hapless debtor into slavery outside Rome and the division of the proceeds of sale among the unpaid creditors. If they preferred, the creditors could kill the debtor and cut him into pieces. The Twelve Tables carefully provided that if a creditor cut more than his share, it should be without liability, thus anticipating Portia's argument against Shylock in Shakespeare's *Merchant of Venice*.

In later times the Romans themselves recognised the primitive features of the law of the Twelve Tables, but it has to be seen in the context of a community which had few resources in terms of state officers who could provide a structure of law enforcement. The legislation provided citizens with a minimum structure within which the parties were left to settle their differences for themselves. Inevitably a party who could call on the assistance of slaves, family and friends was in a stronger position than one with fewer resources at his disposal.

2 LEGAL DEVELOPMENT BY INTERPRETATION

During the course of the republic some features of the Twelve Tables were modified. The creditors of a judgment debtor were no longer allowed to kill him but had to let him work off his debts by forced labour and later there was a procedure for making a debtor bankrupt by a compulsory sale of his property for the benefit of his creditors. But even 500 years after the enactment of the Twelve Tables, the Romans liked to look back on the legislation as what the historian Livy called 'the source of all public and private law', and Cicero says that schoolboys had to learn its contents by heart.

The Romans had a strong feeling that their law was of long standing and had been in essentials part of the fabric of Roman life from time immemorial. At the same time they expected it to enable them to do what they wanted to do, so long as that seemed to be reasonable. In the first half of the republic interpretation of the law, whether the unwritten *ius* or the *lex* of the Twelve Tables, was still in the hands of the pontiffs. They could 'interpret' the law in a progressive way, even to produce a new institution which had been quite unknown to the earlier law.

An example of such interpretation is the emancipation of children from their father's power. The power of the paterfamilias over his descendants in his power lasted until either his or their death. At the time of the Twelve Tables there was no legal means whereby he could voluntarily sever the relationship. He could exploit his sons by selling them into forced labour and the Twelve Tables contained a provision, apparently aimed at curbing misuse of this power, that if the father sold the son three times into forced labour, the son was to be free of his father's power. Such multiple sales were possible because, if the buyer of the son set him free, the son would revert to his father's power.

As a result of interpretation the three-sales rule was used to enable a father to emancipate his son. He made a pretended sale of the son three times to a friend; after each sale the friend would set him free, and after the third he was free by virtue of the Twelve Tables rule. So far the interpretation of the rule can be regarded merely as a use of a clear rule for a purpose other than that originally intended. But interpretation went further. The Twelve Tables referred only to sons; where daughters and grandchildren were concerned the paterfamilias could sell them as much as he liked. Once the rule was understood to refer to emancipation, however, it was held to mean that three sales were required in the case of sons but that so far as daughters and grandchildren were concerned, one sale was sufficient for emancipation.

No doubt many citizens would have seen that what was happening was an adaptation of the Twelve Tables rule for purposes undreamed of by the decemvirs. However, legal conservatives were more comfortable with the idea that emancipation could be presented as something that was at least implicit, if not expressed, in the Twelve Tables than they would have been if it had been proposed as an entirely new reform.

3 THE PRAETOR AND THE CONTROL OF REMEDIES

For most of the duration of the republic the law was developed less through legislation and its interpretation than through the control of legal remedies. Originally the first stage of a legal action was formal and technical; there was a limited number of forms of action, which were begun by the oral declaration of set words in the presence of the magistrate and the defendant. A plaintiff who did not follow the precise wording might lose his action. Such *legis actiones* could only be brought on set days. Once again only the pontiffs were familiar with the exact details until the forms and the calendar were published, traditionally around 300 BC, when the pontificate was opened to the plebeians.

The magistrates, originally the two consuls, elected annually, who replaced the king as the head of the state, were responsible for all governmental activities. The administration of justice was only a minor part of their duties and the procedure allowed them little scope for innovation. As Rome expanded, a special magistrate, called the praetor, also elected annually, was established in 367 BC, to deal exclusively with the administration of justice. He had no special training but he was expected to supervise the formal stage of every legal action. The praetor retained the two-stage character of the legal action, the first concerned with the categorisation of the issue in legal terms and the second with the actual trial of that issue. The second stage had always been, and remained, relatively informal. This procedure was very economical of official time. The magistrate was concerned with the first stage, which was essential, but it was the second stage which was by far the more time-consuming. The Romans realised that in many situations quarrels arise not from disagreement about the law, which is clear enough, but from dispute about the facts and that an ordinary citizen, even without experience of the workings of the law, was quite capable of deciding what had happened.

In the second half of the republic an important change in legal procedure was introduced. When the parties appeared before him, the praetor allowed them, instead of adhering to set forms, to express their claims and defences in their own words. Then, having discovered what the issue was, he set it out in hypothetical terms in a written document, known as a *formula*. This instructed the *iudex* to condemn the defendant, if he found certain allegations proved, and to absolve him, if he did not. The formula, once it was settled by the praetor and the parties, was sealed, so that the *iudex* who opened it could be sure that it had not been tampered with. The *iudex* derived all his authority from the formula and had to act within its terms. So long as he did so, he was allowed great freedom in his conduct of the trial and often took the advice of a *consilium* of friends to help him reach a decision. In the early republic the parties had represented themselves but later they tended to hire professional orators, trained in rhetoric, to present their case to the *iudex*.

The praetor could grant a formula whenever he felt that legal policy justified it, in the sense that he considered that a plaintiff, who could prove his case, ought to have a remedy. The function of the praetors was to declare the law (*ius dicere*) and to give effect to it by their grant of appropriate remedies. Most remedies were concerned with recognised claims, such as that the defendant was detaining the plaintiff's property against his will or that the defendant owed the plaintiff money. The praetor could, however, grant a formula in a situation in which there was no precedent. Officially in such a case he was not making new law; that would have been beyond his powers. In effect he was saying that the claim justified a remedy and so the law must provide it. Although he spoke as if he were just implementing existing law, he was in fact making new law.

Since the new remedies were presented as an expression of the old law, the innovation was disguised. For example, the praetor could not treat as owner of property someone who was not the owner under the civil law, which he was bound to uphold, and so he could not grant such a person the owner's action to recover what was his. He could, however, give a non-owner an alternative action to enable him to obtain physical control of the property, and protect him in that control until he became owner by law through lapse of time. Similarly, he could grant the heir's action to recover the deceased's property only to one who was heir according to the civil law. But he could give a non-heir an alternative remedy to get and keep possession of the property. Such a person enjoyed the property as a possessor rather than as owner. Doubtless for many Romans this was purely a semantic distinction, but for those with an appreciation of the law it was significant. It enabled the praetor to grant a deserving party a remedy, when he felt that the popular sense of justice required it, while at the same time maintaining the formal integrity of the civil law.

At the beginning of his year of office the praetor published an edict, in which he set out the various circumstances in which he would grant a formula, and eventually appended the appropriate formulae. Prospective litigants would consult the edict and could obtain on demand any formula promised in it. A defendant who disputed the plaintiff's allegations would not be prejudiced by the grant of a formula, as he would be confident that his opponent could not persuade the *iudex* that his allegations were well founded.

The formula was a flexible instrument and could be modified to take account of particular defences put forward by the defendant. For example, where the civil law prescribed a particular form for a legal transaction, it was originally concerned only with whether or not the form had been complied with. It did not look behind the form. An important formal contract, mentioned in the Twelve Tables, was *stipulatio*, an oral question-and-answer form which could convert almost any agreement into a binding obligation. If the form had been carried out, the fact that the promisor might have been induced to make his promise by the fraud or threats of the other party was irrelevant. In the later republic, however, the praetor allowed both fraud and duress to be pleaded in the formula by way of a defence to the plaintiff's claim, and if the promisor could prove his assertions, he would be absolved.

Such a defence, or *exceptio*, was required where the defendant admitted the truth of the plaintiff's allegation (e.g. 'I did make the formal promise') but asserted further facts (e.g., 'but that promise was obtained from me by fraud') which nullified the plaintiff's claim. By allowing the defences, the praetor gave legal recognition to the principle that transactions tainted by fraud or duress were unenforceable. In certain formulae, the *iudex* was told to condemn the defendant only to pay whatever sum he ought to pay 'according to good faith (*ex fide bona*)', and in such cases a specific *exceptio* was not needed. The only award which the *iudex* could make at the conclusion of a legal action was money damages. Once he had given his judgment in favour of one of the parties, his task was over and he ceased to exist as a *iudex*. He could not, therefore, order a party to do something or not to do something, since, when the time came to decide whether or not the order had been obeyed, he would no longer be a *iudex*. A decision that a defendant should pay a particular sum is an appropriate conclusion of many types of dispute but it is not suitable in all cases. In the later republic, when remedies other than the grant of regular legal actions were required, the praetor could not remit them to a *iudex* and had to deal with them himself.

The earliest of these 'extraordinary' remedies (i.e., outside the ordinary grant of formulae) was probably the interdict, an order by the praetor to do or not to do something. Many interdicts were designed to prevent interference with the peaceful possession of property and to ensure that claims were made properly by legal process. The praetor did not grant an interdict on demand but would satisfy himself that there was at least some factual justification for making the order. Perhaps the most drastic of these remedies was *restitutio in integrum*. This was the reversal of the legal effect of a transaction, which was formerly valid at civil law but which worked unjustly against one of the parties. Once it had been granted, the parties were given special praetorian actions equivalent to the actions which would have been available to them if the offending transaction had not taken place. The praetor had to show considerable self-restraint in the grant of this remedy. If it were given too widely, it would have undermined public confidence in the law. Why adhere to the forms prescribed for a type of transaction by law if one party can have it set aside because it has effects that he did not foresee? On the other hand, to refuse the remedy altogether would have meant perpetuating injustice. The grounds on which the praetor was prepared to make such an order were carefully chosen. They included fraud, duress, the absence of the complainant on public service for the short period during which another party could possess his land in good faith and become the owner of it by prescription, and the fact that the complainant, although technically an adult, was too young to understand what he was doing.

The last ground further illustrates the cautious Roman approach to law reform. The civil law granted legal capacity to any boy who had reached the age of puberty, eventually agreed to be at fourteen years. At this age he could marry, and if independent of the power of a paterfamilias, deal with his property for himself. This age was quite appropriate in the simple society of the early republic, but a boy of fourteen might well not be able to stand up to a clever merchant, who persuaded him to buy what he did not really want. No doubt the most logical way of dealing with this situation would have been to raise the age of legal capacity. But that would have been seen as a drastic change in a fundamental rule of the traditional law, that capacity and puberty go together.

The Romans were reluctant to contemplate such a change, which might have had all manner of unforeseen consequences. They preferred to leave it to the praetor, in the exercise of his discretion, to reverse the effects of transactions where it appeared that advantage had been taken of the youth's inexperience. The consequence was that people refused to deal with those under the age of twenty-five (the limit set by the praetor), unless they were independently advised.

The law derived from the grant of the new remedies, contained in the edicts of the praetors, was known as *ius honorarium* (from the *honores* held by elected office holders). Most legal development affecting civil disputes in the second half of the Republic was achieved through this kind of law.

4 THE *IUS GENTIUM* AND THE ADVENT OF JURISTS

Where one or both of the parties was not a citizen, it was inappropriate to apply the traditional civil law to their disputes. At first, when non-citizens were relatively rare, the Romans resorted to the fiction that the foreigner was a citizen in order to bring a case within the scope of the civil law. After the Roman victory over the Carthaginians in the Punic Wars of the third century, Roman rule extended over the whole of the western Mediterranean and the number of non-citizens, or peregrines, in daily contact with Romans increased to such an extent that they had to be brought expressly within the ambit of the law. In 242 BC a second praetor was introduced specially to deal with cases in which one or both parties was a peregrine and the two praetors were henceforth distinguished as urban and peregrine.

The civil law was the proud possession of Roman citizens and could not be extended indiscriminately to peregrines. In the third century BC citizenship was a privilege that marked off Romans from other peoples and Romans were expected to observe higher standards of conduct than others. Livy (34.1) records that an Oppian law of 215 BC required Roman matrons to wear simple dress without ornament, while peregrine women walked the streets of Rome in purple and gold. Disputes involving peregrines had, however, to be settled by recognised rules.

The Romans solved the problem in a typically pragmatic way by the recognition that Roman law consisted of two kinds of institutions. There were first those legal institutions, such as traditional ceremonies for the transfer of property from one person to another, which were peculiarly Roman and therefore must be reserved for citizens. There were also other institutions of Roman law, such as many of those derived from praetorian remedies, which were considered to be found in the laws of all civilised people. They collectively formed what the Romans called the *ius gentium*, or law of nations, in contrast with the traditional civil law.

The *ius gentium* was available to citizens and non-citizens alike. The notion enabled the Romans to deal with the practical problem posed by peregrines living under Roman government. Later, when they speculated about why such rules were universally recognised, they suggested that the reason must be that they were based not on traditional practice but on the common sense, or 'natural reason', which all men shared as part of their human nature. Thus the 'law of nations' was sometimes characterised as natural law (*ius naturale*). It came to be accepted that the law of nations and natural law were similar, except for the institution of slavery. This was an institution which was recognised in all ancient societies, and was therefore clearly part of the law of nations, but it was equally clearly not something dictated by common sense and so could not be part of natural law.

In the later republic the formulary system and the supplementary remedies available to litigants became increasingly technical and there was a need for specialist experts to give advice where it was needed. Neither the praetor nor the *iudex*, nor the advocates who represented the parties before them, were trained in the law and all of them needed expert help from time to time. From the second half of the third century we hear of a class of legal experts, jurists, who had no formal role to play in the administration of justice but who were prepared to explain the law to the main players in the legal drama. At first, they were not paid but regarded their work as a form of public service. They took over the function of being custodians of the law from the pontiffs but, unlike the pontiffs, they acted openly and in public.

The work of the Roman jurists was from the beginning concerned with cases which had given rise to legal problems. Their function was to suggest formulae or defences, appropriate for a particular fact-situation, and to draft documents, such as wills or contracts, which would achieve the effect that the parties desired and have no other, undesired, effect. The opinions of these late-republican jurists depended entirely on their personal reputation and those of the more authoritative jurists were collected together in Digests, for reference in similar cases that might arise in the future. The jurists were largely concerned with private law and did not normally deal with public or criminal or religious matters. The law relating to these topics was, as it were, 'factored out' of the civil law, which became synonymous with private law.

5 THE EMPIRE AND THE LAW

The last century of the Roman republic was marked by confusion and conflict between those who wanted to maintain the traditional constitution, even with its weakness of leadership, and those who wanted strong government, even at the cost of dispensing with the legal forms. Matters came to a head with the career of Julius Caesar, who openly flouted the republican forms and was assassinated in 44 BC. The leaders of the conspiracy against him, Brutus and Cassius, were respectively the urban and peregrine praetors at the time.

When the republic was replaced by the empire, the first emperor, Augustus, was anxious to reassure his subjects by preserving the façade of the republican constitution. At first the popular assemblies met as before. Since, however, they had no provision for representation and required the personal presence of the citizens who wished to participate, they consisted in practice of the rabble who lived in the city of Rome itself. The emperors quietly prevented significant proposals for legislation from being put to the assemblies. For a while resolutions of the senate, a body consisting largely of ex-magistrates, acquired the force of law in their place.

The praetorian edict, published annually by successive praetors, had reached the point where it was hardly altered from one year to the next and in the early second century, on the orders of the Emperor Hadrian, it was put into permanent form by the jurist Julian. It begins with the procedure of a formulary action from the summoning of the defendant to the end of the stage before the praetor, covers the various remedies, then the enforcement of judgments after the trial and ends with a section dealing with interdicts and defences. It is likely that this order was modelled on that of the Twelve Tables.

The emperor himself assumed legislative powers and 'imperial constitutions' were now recognised as a source of law with the force of a *lex*. Although the emperors occasionally legislated by edict, the majority of these constitutions were rescripts. They were answers, given in the emperor's name, to questions on the law put by litigants or by public officials, such as provincial governors. The rescripts were drafted by jurists working in the imperial chancery; normally they were concerned to declare and clarify the existing law and very rarely did they introduce significant changes.

By the second century AD, the Roman empire extended from the southern half of Britain, Gaul and the Iberian peninsula in the west, along the west bank of the Rhine and the south bank of the Danube, to Asia Minor, Syria and Egypt in the east. Roman citizenship now became less exclusive than it had been in the republic. By the end of the republic, citizenship had been extended to most of those living in Italy, that is, modern Italy south of the river Po. The imperial government now used the selective grant of citizenship as a means of integrating those living outside Italy into a single whole and thus broke the connection between citizenship and Italian origin.

Increasingly, political, social and economic advancement went to those who were citizens, but now citizenship was compatible with the maintenance of local loyalties, so long as they did not challenge Roman domination. Ambitious provincials were encouraged to acknowledge Rome as a 'common fatherland'. Indeed in the early empire, it was the members of the provincial aristocracies, particularly in the west, such as in Spain, who were the most prominent upholders of the traditional Roman values. The functioning of imperial government came to depend on such men. They served first as army officers and financial agents, then entered the Roman senate, rose to be consul and thereafter governed the military provinces on the frontiers.

Imperial policy encouraged *municipia*, more or less self-governing communities of citizens or Latins (who had many but not all the rights of citizens). A citizen in a provincial *municipium* had a dual status, for each community had a municipal law prescribing in considerable detail how its common life should be organised, with special emphasis on the legal procedure for settling disputes. Although there were variations in detail, we now know that, at least in the western provinces, there was a standard law which was used as a model in most cases, and which as far as possible assimilated the institutions and procedures in the *municipia* to what they were in Rome. The main evidence is an inscription on bronze tablets, discovered in 1981, containing two-thirds of the municipal law of Irni in Spain. Significant parts of the Irni law, which dates from the last quarter of the first century AD, reproduce the text of fragments of other municipal laws that have been known for some time. This identification shows that the institutions at Rome served as a model to which local communities should aspire as nearly as their circumstances allowed. In the eastern Greek-speaking provinces, however, the ancient city-states were less ready to give up their traditional laws.

The first two centuries of the Christian era marked the high point of Roman legal development, in the sense that technically it had reached its most sophisticated and refined form, and the period is known as the classical period of Roman law. These centuries also witnessed some of the most barbaric atrocities of brutal emperors, such as Nero, Caligula and Domitian. There is an apparent paradox that their reigns should be part of the culmination of Rome's glory as a legal state. The answer is to be found in a tacitly accepted distinction that separated private law from other branches of law. Private law concerned the relations between private individuals. The early emperors accepted that there was little advantage to be obtained from interfering with private law and that it was good policy to preserve and develop the private law with no unnecessary change.

6 THE JURISTS IN THE CLASSICAL PERIOD

The main agency of legal development in the classical period was the literature produced by the jurists, both those in the imperial service and those conducting a private practice. The jurists as a class were favoured by the emperors; already Augustus granted to certain jurists the right to give opinions with the emperor's authority, perhaps in order to relieve the pressure created by the demand for rescripts from the imperial chancery. A century later Hadrian laid down that if the opinions of all the jurists with this right were in agreement what they held was to have the force of a *lex*. What this means is not clear, but it may well refer to a practice that had grown up of citing as precedents juristic opinions given in similar cases in the past.

The jurist-law of the classical period was marked by certain characteristics, which may be summarised as follows. First, there was a continuous succession of individuals, all dedicated to the law and each familiar with and building on the efforts of his predecessors, whose views they cited, especially when they agreed with them but sometimes when they disagreed. Secondly, they alone could be said to have a comprehensive knowledge of private law. The praetor held office for only a year, the *iudex* was concerned only with the facts of the cases in which he was chosen to preside and the advocates put skill in argumentation above expertise in law. Indeed, there was a tendency, exemplified by Cicero, who was a successful advocate, to sneer at jurists precisely because they seemed to be immersed in legal minutiae, such as the right to let rain-water from one's roof fall on to one's neighbour's roof. Thirdly, the jurists were concerned with the day-to-day practice of the law and could recognise when modifications or reform of the rules were needed. Although they usually had pupils, they were not academics cut off from 'the real world'. Finally, they enjoyed complete freedom to express divergent opinions. Where legal discussion is concerned with cases, it is inevitably controversial, if only because there are at least two sides to every legal dispute and each side wants a legal opinion in his favour. This is not to say that the jurists twisted the law to suit the client who was consulting them but rather that they were ready to test the limits of every legal rule.

The classical law was thus the product of disputation. The techniques used differed according as the law was in written or unwritten form. Where the jurists were dealing with the text of a *lex* enacted by the republican assembly or of the praetorian edict or the text of a contract or a testament, problems had to be solved by the interpretation given to particular phrases in the text and a number of stock arguments were deployed. Should the strict letter of the text or rather its spirit prevail? Should the actual intention of the author be decisive, even when he has expressed it ambiguously, and, in that case, how should his intention be ascertained? Where the law was in unwritten form, stated in juristic opinions which did not involve a fixed authoritative text, the jurists had more scope for reformulating the law.

In the course of the transmission of our sources, much of the evidence of disagreement has not survived (minority views tend to disappear from the sources), but we do know of the existence of two schools or sects among the jurists in the first and early second centuries AD, known as the Proculians and the Sabinians. There is much scholarly debate about the basis of the differences of these schools, but they seem to have been less concerned with substantive issues than with methods. The Sabinians tended to justify their opinions by referring to traditional practice and to the authority of earlier jurists. They were primarily concerned with finding just solutions in individual cases, even if this meant abandoning logic and rationality. When interpreting texts, they were not worried if the same words were given different meanings in different texts. The Proculians, on the other hand, favoured strict interpretation of all texts and insisted that words and phrases should in every case be given an objective, consistent meaning. In the case of the unwritten law, they assumed that it was a logically coherent system of rules and looked behind the rules for the principles that lay behind them. In that way they could extend the rules by analogy to other cases falling under the same principle. Whatever their affiliation, the jurists distrusted broad statements of principle. This was not because they were unable to formulate them but because they understood that the wider the statement, the more there would be exceptions to its application and so there was a danger that the law would be uncertain and unpredictable.

7 THE ORDERING OF THE LAW

The elaboration of classical law remained largely centred on cases, either real cases or hypothetical cases devised in the schools. Inevitably a casuistic system becomes intricate and complex and in need of categorisation and systematisation. The process of putting the law in some form of order began in the late republic under the influence of Greek methods of classification. The Greeks themselves had not applied these techniques to law, for they had no professional class of jurists and their legal procedure did not lend itself to technical legal development.

About 100 BC the jurist Quintus Mucius Scaevola had published a small treatise on civil law as a whole. It begins with wills, legacies and intestate succession, which occupy about a quarter of the whole work. Problems arising out of the succession to the inheritance of someone who had died produced more disputes than any other kind of case. The social order was based on the family as a unit and the main purpose of a will was to designate the heirs who, on the death of the family head, would take his place and continue the family into the next generation. Apart from nominating his heirs in his will, a testator might grant legacies, appoint tutors for his children under puberty and free slaves. Since property was concentrated in the family rather than in the individual, it is not surprising that succession on death loomed so large in the law. Apart from succession, Mucius grouped the methods of acquiring ownership and possession of property together but the remaining subjects of private law seemed to be jumbled up without any recognisable order.

A century later another jurist, Masurius Sabinus, who gave his name to the Sabinian school, built on Mucius's scheme and brought together other topics, which were beginning to be recognised as having a relationship with each other. For example, Mucius treated theft of property and damage to property as quite separate from each other, but Sabinus brought them together, thus recognising a category of wrongdoing (delict), which gave the victim a civil action for a penalty against the wrongdoer. Sabinus, however, perceived no equivalent category of contract and dealt with the different ways in which two parties could create a binding obligation between themselves quite separately from each other.

Most classical jurists presented their collections of opinions either in the form of a commentary on Sabinus's treatise on the civil law or of a commentary on the (now codified) praetorian edict. It was not until the middle of the second century that a major advance was made in arranging the substance of private law, but it was noticed only in academic circles. The author was an obscure jurist, known simply as Gaius (without the full Roman complement of three names), who was a law teacher. Earlier jurists had had pupils but their main work was concerned with their practice. Gaius, however, seems to have been exclusively a teacher and as such lacked recognition in his own time.

The scheme of his student's manual, the Institutes, is based on a classification of all the law into three parts. Trichotomy was especially attractive to teachers as being a manageable number, suitable for students with a short attention span. The three parts of the law in the Gaian scheme relate to persons, things and actions. The first category was concerned with different kinds of personal status, considered from three points of view, namely, freedom (is the individual a freeman or a slave?), citizenship (is he a citizen or a peregrine?) and family position (is he a paterfamilias or is he in the power of an ancestor?).

The second category, things, bore the main brunt of the classification. It included anything to which a money value could be attributed and comprehended both corporeal and non-corporeal things. Physical things, whether moveable or immoveable, had always been recognised as things. Under the new class of incorporeal things, Gaius put first collectivities of things, which pass *en bloc* (*per universitatem*) from one person to another, such as the inheritance of a deceased person, which passes *en bloc* to his heirs. Such collectivities may include corporeal things but are themselves incorporeal. The other component which Gaius brought under the head of incorporeal things was that of obligations. The notion of obligation had been used to describe the various ways in which one person could become indebted to another and had normally been looked at from the point of view of the person obligated, the debtor. Thus one who entered into a formal promise to another to pay him money became obligated to him; one who received something from another, to secure an existing debt, became obligated to him to return the security when the debt was paid. Sometimes the praetor treated parties as obligated to each other merely on the strength of an agreement reached between them. The main example was an agreement for the sale of goods. Once the parties unconditionally committed themselves to the sale, in that the seller agreed to deliver the thing sold and the buyer agreed to pay the price, they were obligated to each other.

Jurists before Gaius had seen that most obligations were derived from a prior agreement between the parties, even though what made them binding at law might be something more than mere agreement. So most obligations were seen to have a common feature in that, whatever gave them binding force, there had been an agreement between the parties. The category of contracts, imposing duties on the parties, had been born. Gaius now viewed an obligation in a new way; he saw it not just as a burden on the debtor but also as an asset in the hands of the creditor. By treating the creditor's right to sue the debtor as an obligation, Gaius was able to expand the notion of obligations and include in the category not only contracts but also civil wrongs, delicts, as sources of obligations.

The third part of the law in the Gaian scheme was actions. This part was concerned not so much with the procedure for suing in court but rather with the different kinds of action, such as those that can be brought against anyone, as, for example, actions to claim property, in contrast with those that can be brought only against particular individuals, such as actions to enforce obligations.

By the time of Gaius, the heyday of the classical period, the contents of private law were more or less fixed, and he could identify its component elements. His scheme contained several novel features. He included actions among the legal phenomena to be classified, on a par with persons and things; he recognised incorporeal things as falling in the same category as physical things; he classified inheritances and obligations as incorporeal things; and he recognised both contracts and delicts as sources of obligations.

The Institutional scheme was destined to have enormous influence on law in the future but at the time it had little impact outside the schools. The professional jurists did not need a systematic order.

8 THE CULMINATION OF CLASSICAL JURISPRUDENCE

At the beginning of the third century, the Emperor Antoninus Caracalla enacted a significant edict which had the effect of turning most of the residents of his empire into Roman citizens, whether they liked it or not. The *Constitutio Antoniniana* of 212 AD was promulgated not with any liberal intention but probably for fiscal reasons, to apply the inheritance tax levied on the estates of citizens to more people. Another result was that many people who had not considered themselves Roman, and who might not even have known Latin, were now expected, as Roman citizens, to follow the forms of the civil law.

The classical period reached its climax, in the decade after the *Constitutio Antoniniana*, in the work of three jurists whom later ages were to consider the most distinguished, Papinian, Paul and Ulpian. Each of them held the highest imperial office, that of praetorian prefect, and was both the emperor's principal legal officer and his chief of staff. They all wrote prolifically on the law. Papinian excelled in the analysis of particular cases and his solutions to legal problems show a keen moral sense and a desire to reach a just result. Paul and Ulpian are known for their great commentaries, which synthesised the work of their predecessors and passed it on in a mature, but still very complex form, to later generations.

In an elementary institutional work, Ulpian made for the first time a clear distinction between private law and public law. Hitherto the phrase 'public law' had no precise meaning and was often used to indicate those civil law rules which could not be altered by private agreement, by contrast with those that could be altered by the parties. Ulpian now applied the term to the law that was primarily of public concern, such as the powers of magistrates and the state religion, by contrast with the law that concerned the interests of private individuals. What his aim was can only be conjectured but the fact that the work appeared just after the *Constitutio Antoniniana* is significant. Ulpian probably wanted to protect the traditional civil law from imperial interference and to re-assure the new citizens to whom it now applied that the civil law was something quite distinct from public law. The distinction was to have momentous consequences.

With the murder of Ulpian, at the hands of mutinous guards, in 223 AD (Papinian had been executed on the orders of Caracalla a decade earlier), the classical period ended. The second century AD had been a period of unusual peace and stability for the Roman empire. The eighteenth-century historian Edward Gibbon called it 'the period in the history of the world during which the condition of the human race was most happy and prosperous' (*Decline and Fall of the Roman Empire*, ch. 3). The third century, by contrast, was a period of considerable social disorder. Although the imperial rescripts show that efforts were made, at least in the imperial chancery, to maintain the standards of the earlier law, there was little legal writing of the quality needed to justify a claim of vitality in the law.

9 THE DIVISION OF THE EMPIRE

The centre of gravity of the empire was now moving away from Italy and Rome. It was no longer possible to govern it as a single unit. In 284 Diocletian became emperor and undertook a reorganisation of the imperial government. A Dalmatian by origin, he visited Rome for the first time only after he had been emperor for twenty years. He divided the empire into two halves, east and west, each ruled by an Augustus. He chose the east, which he ruled from his capital at Nicomedia in north-western Asia Minor. The provinces were split into smaller units and grouped into thirteen so-called dioceses and they in turn were united into four great prefectures, the governors of the dioceses being the representatives (*vicarii*) of the prefects.

This administrative structure marks the beginning of the process of partition of the empire, with each part having its own emperor. In the early fourth century Constantine built a new capital for the east at Byzantium, or Constantinople, while the western imperial government was based in Milan. Theoretically, however, although the relations of the two parts were sometimes hostile, the empire was still considered to be a single whole, of which the emperors were joint rulers. They struggled to maintain the frontiers of the empire along the Rhine–Danube line, in the face of repeated incursions from Germanic tribes. The latter were themselves being pressed by a general movement westward of other tribes, particularly the dreaded Huns. The defence of the frontier required an army of about half a million men and friendly tribes were allowed by treaty to settle within the empire as *foederati*, on the understanding that they helped to defend it. Large land-owners were obligated to supply soldiers from their estates or else to pay for others to be recruited elsewhere. As a result, many so-called barbarians were recruited into the Roman army and some rose to high command. Unlike the provincials of the first century, these Goths, Franks and Vandals of the fourth century retained their Germanic identity and were not completely romanised.

The Greek speakers of the eastern empire, which had been less affected by barbarian infiltration than the western empire, now began to think of themselves as the prime upholders of the Roman traditions. They called themselves *Rhomaioi* and Constantinople was known as New Rome. In the later fourth century, however, they too began to feel the pressure from the barbarians. In 376 the Visigoths entered Thrace and defeated the eastern imperial army at Adrianople, only 220 km from

Constantinople. The situation was restored by the last great campaigning emperor, Theodosius I, but at the cost of the 'barbarisation' of the eastern army. By an unprecedented treaty in 382 he allowed the Visigoths to settle south of the Danube as a self-governing tribe, with their tribal organisation intact and under their own laws.

On the death of Theodosius in 395, a formal division was created between the two parts of the empire. It was based on the equalisation of resources. Italy, Africa, Gaul, Spain and Britain were clearly in the western part and Thrace, Asia Minor, Oriens and Egypt clearly in the eastern part. The central prefecture of Illyrium was divided between the two: Pannonia (south and west of the Danube in modern Austria and Hungary) was assigned to the west, while Dacia (modern Romania) and Macedonia went to the east. The frontier started at the confluence of the rivers Sava and Danube near Singidunum (modern Belgrade), then went south along the river Drina to the Adriatic and then continued over the Mediterranean to separate Africa from Egypt.

As Edward Gibbon says, 'the respective advantages of territory, riches, populousness and military strength were fairly balanced and compensated in this final and permanent division of the Roman empire' (*Decline and Fall*, ch. 29). This severance of the mainly Greek-speaking east from the Latin west was to have momentous consequences in later centuries. It is still significant in marking the areas of Latin culture in the west from those of Greek, later to be replaced by Slav, culture in the east.

Theodosius's reign also marks the conclusion of another transformation of the empire which began with Constantine, namely its Christianisation. Constantine's Edict of Milan of 313 had ended the official persecution of Christians. Impatient with theological niceties, Constantine made great efforts to unite Christianity, by dealing with the Donatist schism and the Arian heresy, culminating in the Council of Nicaea in 325. Nevertheless the old Roman cults continued at Rome and, until the time of Theodosius, the western emperors accepted the office of *pontifex maximus*. Theodosius, a committed adherent of orthodox catholicism, was much stricter than his predecessors in eliminating paganism and in making catholicism rather than merely Christian belief the official religion. The fact that the Visigoths were staunch Arians compounded his problems in dealing with them.

The new religion hardly affected the supremacy of the emperor initially, since he held himself to be the minister of God for the good of men, but courageous bishops asserted their spiritual power. After Theodosius had ordered the massacre of the citizens of Thessalonica, for lynching the garrison commander, St Ambrose in Milan refused him communion until he had publicly done penance in the cathedral, which he did. Christianity seemed to have little effect, however, on private law. Legislation conflicting with its practice, such as a law of Augustus which penalised celibates in order to increase the birth-rate among citizens, was repealed. But in general the private law of pagan times needed little amendment to fit it for a Christian empire.

10 POST-CLASSICAL LAW AND PROCEDURE

As the government became more bureaucratic, so did legal procedure. The formulary procedure, with the division of the action into two stages, one under the control of a magistrate and the other in the hands of a layman, was abandoned. It was replaced by the *cognitio* procedure, in which the *iudex* was a state-appointed professional judge, who heard the whole case. Orality, which had been a prominent feature of the earlier procedure, now gave way to writing. The plaintiff presented his claim to the court in writing. It was then served by a court officer on the defendant, who filed his defence with the court. The parties appeared before the judge, who heard argument on the legal issues, took proof of fact from witnesses and gave his judgment. If the defendant was condemned, the judgment was enforced by a court officer, unless there was an appeal.

No appeal had been possible against the judgment of a lay *iudex*. The decision of the layman was historically an alternative to a decision based on the ordeal, the judgment of God, and no appeal is possible from the judgment of God. A party who could show that the *iudex* had 'made the cause his own' (*litem suam fecit*) by bias or incompetence could bring an action against him personally but the judgment itself had to stand. Under the new procedure appeals were possible from judges at first instance to higher courts, through the judicial hierarchy up to the court of the emperor himself.

Compared with the formulary procedure, the *cognitio* procedure was profligate of professional time. Junior judges spent a great deal of time hearing and recording evidence and senior judges spent their time hearing appeals. Nevertheless the new procedure, like the governmental structure, was copied by the Church in its own administration and was the forum in which the early canon law developed. It was later to have a decisive influence on continental civil procedure.

Apart from the staff of the imperial chancery (for the flow of rescripts continued unabated) and the judges of the court system, each of the hundred or so provincial governors and each *vicarius* of a diocese needed a legal assessor to advise him. They acted anonymously and, unlike Paul or Ulpian, made no contribution to legal literature. There was no reduction in the number of lawyers but there was a sharp diminution of their quality. The best brains, who had been attracted to law in the second century, turned away from it. The social upheavals of the time were such that clever men preferred to contemplate the heavenly city rather than deal with the problems of the earthly city. The period of legal decline saw the flowering of theological thought represented by patristic literature. Indeed Tertullian, the earliest Latin Church Father, began his career as a lawyer and then abandoned it.

Quite apart from the quality of the personnel involved, the abandonment of the formulary procedure had certain effects on the law. Since it was no longer necessary to choose a particular formula, it was possible to bring an action without identifying precisely what was the legal basis of the claim. Under the earlier procedure the division of function between the praetor and the *iudex* was reflected in a separation of the law from the facts. Now that one judge heard the whole case, that distinction became blurred. The legal issues could gradually emerge as the case proceeded. Technical terms lost their technical meaning and this led to a loss of precision in the law itself.

For example, the classical law made a sharp distinction between ownership and possession. Often the same person both owns and possesses a thing but it is possible to be the owner, in the sense of being entitled to have it, while someone else has physical control of it. The owner who was out of possession had a special action, the *vindicatio*, by which he 'vindicated' what he claimed was his from the person in possession. The latter could not vindicate the thing, although he could seek interdicts which enabled him to resist an attempt by the owner to take the thing directly, instead of proving his entitlement in a *vindicatio*. In the post-classical law the *vindicatio* became an action available to anyone who claimed to be entitled to have the thing in his possession and the distinction between ownership and possession became unimportant.

So also the classical law distinguished between a contract to dispose of property, such as an agreement to sell it, and the actual transfer of ownership from the seller to the buyer. The contract was part of the law of obligations, since it imposed duties on the seller to transfer the property and on the buyer to pay the price, but it had no direct effect on ownership. Until the conveyance, the property remained the seller's and the conveyance was part of the law of physical things. Now that distinction too became blurred and we are told that 'ownership is transferred by a sale'.

To those who appreciate the precision and exact ways of thought characteristic of the classical period, such cases give post-classical law a sloppy, degenerate appearance. It is unscientific and they designate it 'vulgar law', by analogy with the vulgar Latin of the period during which it was being transformed into the separate Romance languages. Others stress that law has to adapt itself to the conditions of the society to which it applies. If they demand more informality at the expense of technicality, that should be seen as a sign of legal vitality and 'organic growth'.

The spread of citizenship throughout the Empire, following on the *Constitutio Antoniniana*, coupled with the relaxation of control of the provinces by the central government, meant that Roman law was now no longer the same everywhere. What had hitherto been a uniform law, applicable to citizens wherever they lived, was becoming provincialised and appeared in different guises in different provinces. The exact extent of the variations is difficult to assess, since the evidence is very patchy for all provinces with the exception of Egypt. There the dryness of the climate has preserved a large quantity of papyri, many of which record legal transactions. They show that the Egyptians tended to follow the local forms, with which they were familiar, and just tacked on a form of words which they hoped would give the document validity in Roman law. In other provinces, where the previous law was less developed, Roman law was probably stronger, but everywhere local variants appeared.

The provincial variants of Roman law were categorised as local custom. Until now the relationship between local custom and general law had not been a great problem. The classical jurists had held that, although frequently law is derived from custom, it only becomes law when it is filtered through one of the recognised sources of law, such as magisterial edict or imperial rescript. Nevertheless a custom of purely local scope could be valid, if it supplemented and did not contradict the law. For example, the law of sale allowed the parties to fix the terms for themselves and provided rules that applied in the absence of specific agreement. Such a rule was that the seller was liable if the buyer were evicted from the thing sold. Normally such liability had to be guaranteed, but the precise extent of the liability, for example, whether the seller should provide not just one surety but two, could be left to local custom. It could be assumed that, unless they stated differently, the parties made the contract with that custom in mind. Such a supplementary custom was therefore valid.

The jurists occasionally speculated about the basis of the authority of such local custom and argued that, just as a statute owes its authority to the will of the people, expressed formally by vote of the popular assembly, so a customary rule owes its authority to the will of the people, expressed by their practice. The second-century jurist Julian held that, since written laws bind us for no other reason than that they have been accepted by the people's judgment, what the people has approved without writing should be equally binding. For what difference does it make whether the people declares its will expressly by vote or by conduct? Julian's text (D.1.3.32), as transmitted to us, ends with the logical conclusion that even written laws may be repealed not only by vote of the legislator but also by the silent agreement of all through 'desuetude', that is, by the adoption of a practice contrary to the written law.

In the third and fourth centuries the extent of local customs increased and the imperial government tried to control the recognition of custom as law in situations where the custom did not merely supplement the law but seemed actually to conflict with it. In 319, the Emperor Constantine recognised that the authority of custom and long usage was significant and could not be overlooked, but that it could be valid only to the extent that it did not override either reason or written law (C. 8.52(53).2).

The difficulty facing those who sought to maintain some consistency in the application of Roman law was that it was often a considerable task to establish just what it was. A fourth-century practitioner would know that he should find the relevant law in writings of authoritative jurists, such as Paul or Ulpian. This was easier said than done, as Paul's commentary on the praetorian edict was in eighty books and Ulpian's in eighty-one books. Earlier jurists would have made frequent consultations of such works and would have made themselves familiar with their contents.

The hard-pressed lawyers of the early fifth century preferred to avoid such consultation, if possible, and relied more on Gaius's Institutes, in which the whole law was set out in only four books. The Institutes and its author gained greatly in prestige in the post-classical period. What the lawyers of the time wanted were rules of thumb, which they could apply without bothering about their rationale. By the middle of the fifth century even Gaius was too complex and an *Epitome Gai* appeared for use in the western empire. The compiler was concerned only with rules and cut out all Gaius's explanations of how those rules had come to have the form that they did.

The lawyers of the time were not really capable of making their own judgment about whose works to consult and what to do when the writings that they consulted disagreed. They wanted imperial direction and this was provided by the Law of Citations of 426 AD, issued in the names of Theodosius II, emperor of the east, and Valentinian III, emperor of the west (both grandsons of Theodosius I). The Law elevated five jurists to the status of primary authorities: Papinian, Paul, Ulpian, Modestinus and Gaius. The first three, the giants who dominated the last phase of classical law, practically chose themselves and Modestinus, a pupil of Ulpian, was the last jurist of note. The significant feature of the list is the inclusion of Gaius, which demonstrates the popularity of his works in the post-classical period. The law also allowed reference to secondary works cited by the five primary authorities, but since manuscripts of their works would be scarce and unreliable, such reference required comparison of manuscripts. In practice, therefore, it was only the five jurists who counted. If their opinions differed, the majority view should be accepted. If the numbers were equal, Papinian's view prevailed. Only if the numbers were equal and Papinian was silent could the judge make up his own mind on the matter. The reduction of law-finding to a purely mechanical process is testimony to the fact that Roman legal science had reached its nadir.

The law found in juristic writings was now referred to as *ius*, in contrast with that derived from imperial legislation, for which the designation was *lex*. The spate of imperial enactments required ordering and systematisation. Two private collections of imperial constitutions, mostly rescripts, were made at the end of the third century, called *Codex Gregorianus* and *Codex Hermogenianus*, after their compilers. In the fifth century the imperial authorities felt that an official compilation was required and in 429 Theodosius II appointed a commission to make a collection of all imperial legislation enacted since the time of Constantine.

The original plan contemplated a second collection which would combine legislation and juristic writing into a grand plan of life for all the citizens of the empire (C.Th.1.1.5). As the work proceeded, however, the inclusion of juristic writings was abandoned and the compilers were permitted to abbreviate and alter the text of the laws they included, so that they should state the law actually in force. The whole compilation in sixteen books, with the laws arranged in titles in chronological order, was completed early in 438. The work was conceived and executed in the eastern empire but copies were sent to the west, where it was approved by the Emperor Valentinian III and the senate.

The original text of the Theodosian Code has not survived but it has been substantially reconstructed. It is a major source for the political and economic history, as well as for the legal history, of the late empire but it is not easy to use, as the language is grandiloquent and often obscure. Its constitutions seem to have been drafted by imperial officials who felt that it was more important that imperial legislation should reflect the splendour of the imperial office than that it should be intelligible to those who had to follow its precepts. In the west, at least, it had to be supplemented by *interpretationes*, to explain its contents in simple language.

II THE END OF THE WESTERN EMPIRE

During the fifth century the western empire gradually disintegrated in the face of continuous pressure from Germanic tribes. At the beginning of the century, the Visigoths under Alaric moved westward, entered Italy and were only temporarily kept at bay by troops withdrawn from the defence of Britain, which was being invaded by Saxons. The western imperial government at Milan was now transferred to Ravenna, near the Adriatic. In 410 the Visigoths sacked the city of Rome. It had long ceased to be an administrative or military centre, but its ancient traditions, the fact that the senate still met there and its growing importance as the papal seat gave it enormous symbolic value. Shock-waves spread through the empire at the news. St Jerome, whose origins were on the boundary of Italy and Illyria, writing from Bethlehem, exclaimed in horror that the brightest light of the whole earth had been extinguished and the empire deprived of its head (preface to Commentary on Ezekiel, 1). The legal life of Italy did not recover from the war. In a constitution of 451 Valentinian III laments the fact that certain regions lacked both advocates and judges and that those who knew the law were to be found rarely or not at all (*Nov. Val.* 32.6).

Two years after the sack of Rome, the Visigoths moved into south-western Gaul, south of the Loire, where they were allowed by treaty to establish themselves with a capital at Toulouse. In eastern Gaul the Burgundians were permitted to settle on similar terms and make common cause with the Gallo-Roman inhabitants against the Huns.

Their capital was Worms. In 429 the Vandals, who had passed through Gaul into Spain, landed in Africa and soon established an independent kingdom within the imperial frontiers. In 455 they too invaded Italy and sacked Rome. Finally in 476 the last Roman emperor in the west gave up his throne and the Germanic kingdoms in Gaul and Spain became as independent in theory as for some time they had been in practice. To some extent the vacuum created at the centre of the western empire by the collapse of imperial government was filled by the Church. When the secular administration failed, the ecclesiastical administration, which largely mirrored that of the empire, took its place. Pope Leo I (440–61) negotiated both with Attila, the Hun leader, and Gaiseric, the Vandal leader. He built on the fact that Roman Christians in the western provinces were Catholic to secure the primacy of the see of Rome. According to Leo, the Bishop of Rome, as successor of St Peter, transmitted apostolic authority to all other bishops, who were therefore subordinate to him. This doctrine even found favour with many bishops of the eastern empire, despite the fact that they accorded the bishop of Constantinople the same precedence as the bishop of old Rome.

In a letter to the eastern Emperor Anastasius in 494, Pope Gelasius I put forward the view that the world is governed by two separate authorities, *sacerdotium* and *imperium*, that of the Pope in matters spiritual and that of the emperor in matters temporal, both being subject to the lordship of Christ. He claimed for the papacy, against other bishops, the ultimate right to try cases affecting the Church. The Church was beginning to develop its own legal system, based on resolutions of Church councils, the Bible and papal decisions, known as decretals. What welded these disparate sources into a single whole was the Roman secular law, from which the Church lawyers derived their basic categories.

The newly independent Germanic tribes were always heavily outnumbered by their romanised subjects and were usually glad to leave them to maintain their existing legal institutions. They followed the principle of personal law and, whereas they retained their own laws for themselves, they did not seek to impose them on others. The more advanced of these peoples felt the need to have their tribal laws put into written form. Significantly they did not publish them in their own languages but in Latin, the language of administration and law. They used Gallo-Roman scribes, familiar with the vocabulary of Roman law, and it would have been difficult for them, even if they had wished to do so, to keep the substance of what they were writing immune from the technical meaning of the expressions in which it was expressed.

The first known example of such legislation is in the form of an edict promulgated by Euric, king of the Visigoths from 466 to 484. It was probably published about 475, when Euric was asserting the authority hitherto exercised by the Roman prefect of Gaul. Instead of recording agreed Visigothic practice in the manner of traditional Germanic laws, Euric's law was formulated, in the manner of imperial constitutions, by the king and the chief magnates of his realm. Euric wanted to keep his Roman and Visigothic subjects apart and forbade intermarriage between them but there are several instances of the direct influence of Roman law, for example, a clause forbidding actions concerning matters which occurred more than thirty years previously. The draftsmen of Euric's law, being trained in Roman law, tended to see Roman law as expressing basic principles, which should lie behind the laws of all peoples. They recognised that there must be a temporal limit to litigation on any private dispute and inserted the Roman rule.

Three collections of specifically Roman law for the subjects of barbarian rulers appeared at the beginning of the sixth century. The Edict of Theodoric was promulgated about 500 by Theodoric the Great, king of the Ostrogoths in Italy, who found it politically convenient to regard himself as the representative of the eastern emperor in Constantinople. His Edict applied to both Romans and Goths but the material is Roman. Although the sources are not specified, they are the Theodosian Code of imperial legislation and its two predecessors, with post-Theodosian 'Novels' (*novellae constitutiones*), the Sentences of Paul (probably an early post-classical selection of short opinions of the master) and Gaius's Institutes.

The Burgundian and Visigothic kings in Gaul promulgated separate collections of legal materials, specifically intended for the 'Romans' in their dominions. The Burgundian kingdom had been re-established further south than their original settlement on the Rhine but was in a vulnerable position, squeezed between the Franks to the north, the Visigoths to the west and the Ostrogoths to the east. King Gundobad of the Burgundians enacted two laws. One, variously called Lex Burgundionum, Lex Gundobada, Loi Gombette and Book of Constitutions, was exclusively for Burgundians. The parallel law, the 'Lex Romana Burgundionum', is similar in form to the Edict of Theodoric and is derived from the same sources.

The most influential of these collections of Roman materials was the 'Lex Romana Visigothorum', otherwise known as the Breviary of Alaric. It was published by Alaric II, king of the Visigoths, in 506 for his Roman

subjects, perhaps as an attempt to ensure their loyalty in the face of
attack by the Franks (with whom Gundobad's Burgundians were allied).
This resulted in the defeat of the Visigoths at Vouglé, near Poitiers, in
507 and the subsequent concentration of the main part of their kingdom
in Spain. Again the same sources were used as those of the Edict of
Theodoric and the 'Lex Romana Burgundionum' but this time they are
expressly cited and the material is more extensive. A distinction is made
between *lex* (official legislation) and *ius*. There are selected constitutions
from the Theodosian Code and post-Theodosian Novels, followed by
extracts from the Sentences of Paul and the complete *Epitome Gai*, the
Gallic version of Gaius's Institutes. There are also extracts from the two
pre-Theodosian codices, which, since they were private, unofficial collections, are treated as *ius* rather than *lex*. Finally there is a single fragment from Papinian, clearly inserted on account of the reputation of
that jurist. Each part of the collection, with the exception of the *Epitome
Gai*, is furnished with *interpretationes*, giving the gist of the text in succinct,
robust Latin. These comments were probably taken from materials produced in Gallic schools of law in the previous century.

   The Visigothic Roman law is our main source for western vulgar law
in the last century of the western empire. It also became the main source
for Roman law in the kingdoms which replaced the empire from the
sixth century to the eleventh. It was in force in the Visigothic kingdom
in Spain until the middle of the seventh century, when the fusion of the
two peoples was recognised and the law became territorial, applicable to
all living in the kingdom, rather than personal. In practice the Visigothic
collection also maintained its authority in the kingdom of the Franks
which, after their defeat of the Visigoths in 507 and of the Burgundians
in 532, extended over the whole of former Gaul. The Franks accepted
the personality principle but published no compilation of Roman law,
preferring instead to use the Visigothic and the Burgundian Roman
laws, which were often copied together in Frankish manuscripts.

12 JUSTINIAN AND THE CORPUS IURIS

The collapse of the western empire had left the eastern empire relatively unscathed and indeed the second half of the fifth century saw a
revival of legal learning in the law schools of Constantinople and
Beirut. The texts were, of course, all in Latin but they were expounded
in Greek. In 527 there ascended the imperial throne a man whose name
is for ever associated with Roman law. Justinian was born near Naissus

(Niš in modern Serbia), also the birthplace of Constantine. He was a native Latin-speaker (the last eastern emperor to be such) but enjoyed a Greek education at Constantinople, which now reverted to its old name of Byzantium. His legal work was part of an ambitious programme to renew the ancient glory of the Roman empire in all its aspects. A man of great nervous energy and command of detail, like Napoleon he required little sleep. He was much influenced by his wife Theodora, a former actress, and after her death in 448, he was less active as a ruler. Through the efforts of his generals, Narses and Belisarius, he recovered North Africa from the Vandals and re-established imperial authority over the Ostrogothic kingdom in Italy. He resisted the claims of the Pope to equal authority with the emperor and regarded himself as holding supreme religious as well as supreme temporal power. The symbol of his religious authority was the great church of Hagia Sophia in Byzantium, in the building of which he claimed to have surpassed Solomon.

In his legal work Justinian was fortunate in having a brilliant minister, Tribonian, to execute his plans. Whether his ideas were influenced by what the Visigothic king had done, it is not possible to say, for Justinian would never have admitted it. Whereas Alaric's aim was to give his Roman subjects a law suitable for sixth-century Gaul, Justinian consciously looked back to the golden age of Roman law and aimed to restore it to the peak it had reached three centuries before. Rather inconsistently he also wanted a law that could be applied in the Byzantine empire of his own time.

One part of his project was modest enough: to bring the Theodosian Code up to date. The main agency of legal development had been imperial constitutions and there had been many 'Novels' in the previous century. Justinian's Code arranges the constitutions in chronological order in titles and covers twelve books. In the course of the general overhaul of the law, many controversies, unresolved since the time of the classical jurists, came to light and were settled by his own constitutions.

The most important part of Justinian's compilation was quite unprecedented. This is the Digest (Latin *Digesta*; Greek *Pandectae*), an anthology of extracts from the writings of the great jurists. The five jurists of the Law of Citations are given pride of place, over one-third of the Digest being taken from Ulpian and a sixth from Paul, but there are extracts from earlier jurists of repute, even the jurists of the late republic. The whole forms an immense legal mosaic, about one and a half times the size of the Bible, but it represents, Justinian says, only a twentieth of the material with which its compilers began. The extracts are arranged in titles, each title being devoted to a particular topic and the titles arranged in fifty books. Where a subject could not easily be divided up, such as legacies, a single title might extend over three books. Normally, however, division was preferred, as with the contract of sale which is covered in eight titles: a general title and special titles dealing with particular aspects of sale. The order of the titles is the traditional order of the praetorian edict, but the fragments within each title seem to be arranged quite haphazardly.

The compilers were instructed to attribute each fragment to its source by an appropriate inscription. In the nineteenth century, the German scholar Bluhme showed, from a study of these inscriptions, that extracts from particular works appear in three groups and that within each group the extracts normally appear in the same order, although the groups themselves were not arranged in the same order in every title. He therefore concluded that the compilers, under pressure from the emperor to speed up the work, must have divided themselves into three committees, each of which took a bundle of works to extract. They then brought chains of fragments to a plenary session, at which the order of the respective chains was agreed for each title and a few specially significant fragments moved out of order into a more prominent position. Recent research, based on computerised study of the text, has further refined Bluhme's conclusions.

The Digest was produced in three years and the compilers must have had their work cut out just abbreviating the material at their disposal and making the resulting extracts as coherent as possible. Although they gave the source of each extract, we cannot assume that what they attributed to the jurist is what he actually wrote. This is partly because the original discussion has been cut down, but also because the compilers were expressly instructed to eliminate all contradictions and to avoid repetitions. Much evidence of disagreement among the classical jurists was therefore excised.

The compilers were also authorised to make whatever substantive changes were necessary to ensure that the final work expressed the law of sixth-century Byzantium. It is the extent of such alterations which has been a main concern of Digest study in the twentieth century. The changes in the texts have been known since the sixteenth century as *emblemata Triboniani* and more recently as interpolations, whether they subtract from, add to, or just alter the original text.

The Code and the Digest are the main parts of Justinian's compilation, but they were too complex to put into the hands of students at the beginning of their studies, and Justinian ordered that they be supplemented by a new Institutes, based on Gaius's Institutes of nearly four centuries earlier. Although an elementary text-book, it was given equal status with the Digest and Code. The Digest and Institutes became law on 31 December 533 and a revised edition of the Code a year later.

The materials out of which Justinian's compilation was forged were of differing origin, some, the contents of the Code, being derived from legislation and others, the juristic writings, enjoying only the authority derived from the author's reputation. Justinian made the whole work his own, converting it into statutory form. Defending the changes that had been made in his name, he observed that he who corrects what is not stated accurately deserves more praise than the original writer (*Constitutio Deo auctore*, 6). He prohibited any reference to the original material and tried to ban commentaries on the text on the ground that it was crystal clear as it stood.

Justinian continued to issue constitutions until his death in 565. These Novels, many of them written in Greek, were collected together privately and added to the other three parts of what came to be called the Corpus iuris civilis, the body of the civil law, by contrast with the canon law of the Church. The whole collection marked the culmination of a millennium of legal development. Without Justinian's compilation we would know very little about the earlier law. Little classical law has survived directly, the main example being Gaius's Institutes, the full text of which was discovered only in 1816.

The extraordinary fact about Justinian's work is that, despite the fanfare with which it was published, it attracted relatively little attention. Being written in Latin, it was unintelligible to many Greek-speaking Byzantine lawyers. One of the compilers of the Institutes, Theophilus, produced a Greek version of that work known as the Paraphrase. In the eighth century a shorter official collection in Greek appeared, called the *Ecloga*, which sought to modify Justinian's law in the direction of current Byzantine practice. About 900 Emperor Leo the Wise sponsored a large Greek restatement of Justinian's law, the *Basilica*, which wove the contents of Digest, Code, Institutes and Novels into a single whole. The texts were supplemented with scholia, notes mainly derived from the comments of the jurists of Justinian's own time and therefore sometimes of value in elucidating the original Latin text. Shorter versions of the *Basilica* were produced in the following centuries, the most influential being the *Hexabiblos* (six-book work), published in 1345, which was still recognised as the basis of the law of modern Greece until replaced by the code of 1940.

In 1453 the Byzantine empire, which had been gradually contracting in size, finally succumbed to Turkish attack, but Byzantine Roman law in Greek dress survived in the Balkans and in Russia, whose emperors liked to regard themselves as the successors of the Byzantine emperors.

FURTHER READING

Bibliographical references are grouped under the relevant chapter and section number. For the development of ancient Roman law in general, see H. F. Jolowicz and B. Nicholas, *Historical Introduction to the Study of Roman Law*, 3rd edn, Cambridge 1972; W. Kunkel, trans. J. M. Kelly, *An Introduction to Roman Legal and Constitutional History*, Oxford 1966; A. A. Schiller, *Roman Law: Mechanisms of Development*, The Hague, Paris, New York 1978; B. Nicholas, *An Introduction to Roman Law*, 3rd edn, Oxford 1988. For the text and translation of all Roman statutes from the Twelve Tables, M. H. Crawford (ed.), *Roman Statutes*, 2 vols., London 1996. A translation of the Twelve Tables, Praetor's Edict and other sources is in A. C. Johnson, P. R. Coleman-Norton and F. C. Bourne, *Ancient Roman Statutes*, Austin, Tex. 1961. For the later empire, Edward Gibbon, *Decline and Fall of the Roman Empire, 1776–88*, is still valuable, to be supplemented by A. H. M. Jones, *The Later Roman Empire, 284–602*, 3 vols., Oxford 1964.

2.1. P. Stein, *Regulae iuris: From Juristic Rules to Legal Maxims*, Edinburgh 1966.

2.5. A. N. Sherwin-White, *The Roman Citizenship*, 2nd edn, Oxford 1973; J. Gonzalez, 'The Lex Irnitana: a new Flavian municipal law', *Journal of Roman Studies*, 76 (1986), 147.

2.6. B. Frier, *The Rise of the Roman Jurists*, Princeton 1985; A. A. Schiller, 'Jurists' Law', *An American Experience in Roman Law*, Göttingen 1971, 148.

2.7. P. Stein, 'The development of the Institutional system', in P. Stein and A. Lewis (eds.), *Studies in Justinian's Institutes in Memory of J. A. C. Thomas*, London 1983, 151; *The Institutes of Gaius*, with trans. by W. M. Gordon and O. Robinson, London 1988.

2.8. T. Honoré, *Ulpian*, Oxford 1982; P. Stein, 'Ulpian and the distinction between *ius publicum* and *ius privatum*', *Collatio iuris romani, études dédiées à Hans Ankum*, Amsterdam 1995.

2.10. E. Levy, *West Roman Vulgar Law: The Law of Property*, Philadelphia 1951; *Weströmisches Vulgarrecht* II: *Das Obligationenrecht*, Weimar 1956.

2.11. *The Theodosian Code and Novels*, trans. with commentary by C. Pharr, Princeton, London 1952; T. Honoré, 'The making of the Theodosian Code', *ZSS (RA)*, 103 (1986), 133.

2.13. The standard edition of the Corpus iuris civilis is I: *Digesta*, ed. T. Mommsen and P. Krueger, 16th edn, Berlin 1954; II: *Codex*, ed. P. Krueger, 11th edn, Berlin 1954; III: *Novellae*, ed. R. Schoell and G. Kroll, 6th edn, Berlin 1954. The Digest text is reprinted with English translation in *The Digest of Justinian*, ed. A. Watson, 4 vols., Philadelphia 1985; that of the Institutes with trans. by P. Birks and G. McLeod, London 1987. For the compilation, T. Honoré, *Tribonian*, London, 1978; D. Osler, 'The compilation of Justinian's Digest', *ZSS (RA)* 102 (1985), 130.

CHAPTER 3

The revival of Justinian's law

I ROMAN LAW AND GERMANIC LAW IN THE WEST

From the sixth century until the eleventh, a reference to Roman law in Western Europe was normally understood to be to the law of the so-called barbarian codes, in particular the Roman law of the Visigoths. These collections reflected not Roman law of the classical period but the 'vulgar law' of the fifth century. They served as quarries from which rules could be dug when required for smaller collections. Compared with the scope and complexities of Justinian's compilation, their contents reflected a low level of legal science, but even so they sometimes proved to be beyond the comprehension of those who consulted them in the sixth and seventh centuries.

In the early middle ages, the imperial system of courts, staffed by professional judges who represented a state machine that could enforce their decrees, disappeared. In its place were groups of freemen from the locality who sought to settle disputes in such a way that the disruption of community life would be minimised. The assemblies of freemen had to establish the customary rules relevant to the case before them. These rules were not applied rigidly but provided a background against which the dispute was to be settled, often by compromise. Instead of the sense of belonging to a world empire, the individual had more of the sense of being part of a community of people of similar ethnic origin with similar customary traditions.

Where the parties could not be reconciled, the community courts decided on the method of proof, often leaving vital points to be established by the 'judgment of God'. This was ascertained by ordeals, by battle or by the production of oath-helpers, who swore to their belief in the truth of their party's assertions; the party producing the larger number of oath-helpers won the case. The final judgments were enforced by community pressure, with the ultimate threat of being 'outlawed' from the community.

It is in this context that the law in the early middle ages must be considered. It is misleading to think of a sharp division between Roman law, on the one hand, and the Germanic customary laws, on the other. The courts would attempt to make the parties recognise the traditional rules that applied in the communities to which they belonged, but they were free in unusual cases to cite relevant rules taken from other tribal laws or from Roman law. In the sixth century, Roman law was still applied to the affairs of the 'Roman', that is, the Gallo-Roman, subject peoples of the Germanic conquerors, but gradually, with the fusion of populations, the personal principle gave way to the territorial principle, by which all those living in a particular area were subjected to the same law.

The law that prevailed in this period was essentially the Germanic custom of the rulers, which hitherto had been orally transmitted but now was collected together and recorded in writing. As in the case of Euric's law, the authorities enlisted the aid of the Gallo-Roman lawyers and scribes and the language of the text was Latin. These laws were concerned mainly with the money compositions that were payable to the victim or the victim's family in respect of various offences, such as theft, damage to property, personal injury, sexual offences and homicide. The rules in this regard were very detailed, specifying precise penalties which reflected the relative significance of different kinds of theft or injury, and show little Roman influence. There were some rules on family status and on procedure but very few on contracts and property.

From the eighth century, traces of Roman influence in the substance of the Germanic laws are more noticeable but often the Roman texts were not understood. The 'Lex Romana Curiensis' was a collection made at the end of the eighth century for the romanised population of Rhaetia in eastern Switzerland. It contains a reference to the Law of Citations of 426, which provided that when juristic opinions were cited in court, the judge should follow the majority view and, if the numbers were equal, the view of Papinian should prevail. This rule was understood by the eighth-century lawyers to refer to the practice whereby each party produced oath-helpers in court, with the majority prevailing. If the numbers on each side were equal, it was now said, the party who could cite some title in the 'lex Papianus' in his support, should win the case. Papianus was an early medieval designation of the 'Lex Romana Burgundionum', because in some manuscripts it followed the Roman law of the Visigoths and was thought to be a continuation of the fragment of Papinian which concluded the latter collection.

In Italy a better comprehension of Roman law survived and the Edict of the eighth-century Lombard king Liutprand indicates that reference was being made to Roman law in commercial matters, which were hardly touched on by Germanic laws. Where, as in Lombardy, there was a strong tradition of reliance on formal written documents to attest transfers of property and the creation of debts, the relevant deeds were normally prepared by professional notaries, who adhered to the traditional formularies. Liutprand's Edict provides that written documents made before Roman notaries had to conform to the rules of Roman law and Lombard deeds had to conform to the rules of Lombard law; one party to a transaction, however, with the consent of the other party, might give up his personal law and follow another. This must refer to a practice which had grown up to avoid the inconveniences of the personal principle, where a transaction involved parties from different communities.

Italy was an exception to the rule that Roman law meant exclusively the law of the barbarian codes. In 553, at the end of a long and disastrous war with the Ostrogothic kingdom, Justinian's generals had briefly brought the whole of Italy under Byzantine rule and the following year, 'at the request of Pope Vigilius', Justinian promulgated the 'pragmatic sanction' providing for the extension of his compilation to Italy. Even after the Lombard invasion in 568 certain parts of the peninsula, especially the south, much of which was Greek-speaking, and the region of Ravenna, seat of the Byzantine exarch, maintained regular contacts with the Byzantine empire. As a result, parts of Justinian's law, other than the Digest, were known and used in parts of Italy. These were Justinian's Institutes, the first nine books of the Code (the last three books were concerned with Byzantine administrative law) and a sixth-century Latin abbreviation of Justinian's Novels, known as the *Epitome Juliani* and intended to be applied in Italy.

The main custodian of the Roman legal tradition was the Church. As an institution, the personal law of the Church throughout Europe was Roman law. In the words of the law of the Ripuarian Franks (61 (58)1), 'the Church lives by the Roman law'. The Church continued to build up its own special law in collections of relevant texts. As the problems facing the Church increased in complexity, so the references to Roman law increased. Broad statements of principle were specially prized but there was specific material dealing with the ecclesiastical matters, such as the legal status of monks, especially in the Novels. The Roman material relevant to the Church was brought together in particular collections, such as the 'Lex Romana canonice compta' of the ninth century.

The level of legal expertise was highest in Italy, but the Church carried some knowledge of Roman legal notions even to remote parts of Europe, where Roman institutions had disappeared after the end of imperial rule. The Anglo-Saxon kingdoms in England did not make any special legal provision for what remained of their Gallo-Roman subjects. After the evangelisation of England from Rome in the seventh century, however, the Church did not confine its teaching to the Gospel. We hear of teaching on a variety of subjects, including Roman law, at the school set up by Theodore of Tarsus in Canterbury. Some idea of the substance of such instruction may be derived from Theodore's *Poenitentiale*, which contains the master's answers to legal problems about such topics as the requirements for a marriage, the status of slaves and compensation for injuries. They show both some knowledge of Roman law and a determination to apply it. Some of these rules later found their way into the Anglo-Saxon laws themselves. Purist Christian writers, such as the Venerable Bede, objected to Roman law because of its secular, non-Christian character. As a significant part of the learning of antiquity, however, it retained a foothold in most cathedral schools and monastic libraries.

Although there is no evidence of serious study, it was felt that at least some familiarity with Roman law, as an integral part of the Roman heritage, was a necessary part of a sound education, especially of churchmen. A major source of reference for elementary Roman law throughout Europe outside Italy was the encyclopedic *Etymologiae* of St Isidore of Seville, written in the 620s. St Isidore's knowledge of the subject was derived from the vulgar law of the western empire and, in listing the great legislators, he does not mention Justinian. The number of surviving manuscripts throughout Europe demonstrates that it was to this work especially that literate clerics went to find the meaning of technical legal terms and abbreviations.

2 CHURCH AND EMPIRE

In 774 the Frankish king, Charlemagne, overthrew the Lombards and installed his son as king in the Lombard capital, Pavia. Charlemagne was influenced by the Anglo-Saxon scholar Alcuin of York, whom he met in Parma in 781 and made royal tutor and adviser on educational and religious matters. Alcuin revived the memory of Rome as *caput mundi* and this idea became a dominant feature of the so-called Carolingian Renaissance. On Christmas Day 800 Charlemagne sought to realise Alcuin's vision when he had himself crowned emperor at Rome by Pope

Leo III and thus reconstituted his different kingdoms into a new empire. Both emperor and Pope exploited the mystical memory of Rome and her universal empire. The Roman crowd acclaimed Charlemagne as 'crowned by God' and he could thus call his empire both 'Holy' and 'Roman'.

There was now renewed interest in the relationship between Church and empire. In the spirit of the letter of Pope Gelasius I to the Emperor Anastasius in 494, the Popes had issued decretals with general application. Now Charlemagne and his successors claimed the power to make laws, without popular consent, for all their subjects, irrespective of their nation, on the model of the Roman imperial law. Their 'capitularies' formed a general territorial law, by contrast with the personal tribal laws, and was the first body of law to be designated as *ius commune*. The notion was attractive, since in many parts of the continent the various tribes had begun to fuse together and their Germanic languages were giving way to dialects of Latin.

In the tenth and eleventh centuries the equilibrium postulated by the Gelasian principle of two separate authorities, vested in Pope and emperor, was disturbed by the struggles between Church and empire, in which the papal lawyers argued that its divine mission made the Church superior to the empire, so that imperial law was only valid if it conformed with Church law. Each side appealed to Roman law to justify its position. The texts of Justinian's Code did not assist the Church. Justinian had rejected the Gelasian principle. He had held that the emperor united in himself not only the supreme temporal power, expressed in the notion of *imperium*, but also the supreme spiritual power of *sacerdotium*. In the opening fragment of the Code he announced that all peoples under his rule must practise the orthodox faith that St Peter had transmitted to the Romans. However, the leading Church lawyer at the end of the eleventh century, St Ivo of Chartres, argued that the fact that the compilations of what was now being called canon law included only particular Roman rules showed that Roman law was only applicable to the extent that it had been accepted by the Church.

Matters came to a head with the declaration by Pope Gregory VII in 1075 prohibiting lay investiture, the claim of the emperor and other princes to invest an abbot or bishop with the ring and staff of his office. This declaration was effectively an affirmation of the independence of the Church and of its higher clergy from all secular states. The investiture controversy rumbled on for half a century and symbolised the struggle between Church and empire for dominance. It provided a stimulus to both sides to find legal arguments to support their case and gave both sides a sense that the whole of Europe was affected.

The controversy was formally concluded by Pope Callixtus II and the Emperor Henry V in the Concordat of Worms in 1122, based on an earlier compromise made with King Henry I of England. The concordat made a distinction between the spiritual office of a prelate and his position as a feudal vassal of the Crown and provided that he should do homage to the emperor for his feudal powers and then receive his ring and staff, as the symbols of his spiritual authority, from his ecclesiastical superior. Soon after the compromise had been reached, Callixtus wrote to Henry V of 'how much loss the discord between Church and Empire had brought to the Faithful of Europe and how much our peace and unity would bear fruit' (*Monumenta Germaniae Historica*, Const. 1.110). There was thus a sense of Europe as a Christian entity, ruled by Pope and emperor, and of the need to maintain its unity, but henceforth it was to be a Europe with two regimes, each with its own set of laws.

3 THE REDISCOVERY OF THE DIGEST

In the later eleventh century the level of legal culture began to rise and there is evidence of a new interest in Justinian's law; notaries in their documents and advocates in their pleadings now refer accurately to technical Roman legal institutions. Five hundred years after its compilation, Justinian's Digest came to be used in Western Europe as a source of rules and arguments. No doubt there had been manuscripts lurking in Italian libraries but their bulk and the difficulty of understanding them had hitherto deterred potential readers. All surviving manuscripts of the Digest today derive ultimately from a sixth-century codex in Pisa, which was seized as war booty by the victorious Florentines in 1406 and is now in the Laurentian library in Florence. The relationship is not direct but through a lost, amended, copy made in the eleventh century and known as *Codex secundus*. This version was the source of the *vulgata* or *litera bononiensis*, that came to be studied in the twelfth-century schools.

The recovery of the entire Corpus iuris civilis was a slow process, extending over much of the twelfth century. The Digest became available in three parts, known as *Vetus*, *Infortiatum* and *Novum*. The division bears little relation to the original structure, *Vetus* being Books 1 to 24.2, *Infortiatum* Books 24.3 to 38 and *Novum* Books 39 to 50. The origin of the division, and in particular the designation *Infortiatum* for the middle section, is unknown and was a mystery to the twelfth-century doctors themselves. It probably reflects the order in which the parts of the Digest became generally available. Eventually the complete Digest could be added to the Institutes and to the first nine books of the Code. Later the *Tres libri* (the last three books of Justinian's Code) were discovered but were kept separate rather than integrated into the rest of the Code; and a better version of the Novels than the *Epitome Juliani*, known as the *Authenticum*, became available. The latter was grouped into nine *Collationes* in imitation of the Code. The Institutes, *Tres libri*, and *Authenticum* were placed in a fifth volume, after the three volumes of the Digest and the (nine books of the) Code. This so-called *volumen parvum* formed a receptacle, which also incorporated some non-Justinian material, such as twelfth-century imperial legislation.

The churchmen were perhaps even more eager than secular lawyers to exploit the newly discovered texts to justify the new ideas that church-men were proposing. Ninety-three extracts from the Digest, ninety of them from the *Digestum vetus*, appear in a canonist collection known as *Collectio Britannica*, an Italian work from about 1080, now known only in a single manuscript in the British Library. The immediate source of these Digest texts is not known but the compilers may well have found them in archives in Rome or perhaps in the great Benedictine monas-tery of Monte Cassino. The French canonist Ivo of Chartres is known, for example, to have been working on his own collections in Rome in the 1090s. The *Collectio Britannica* itself became the source of local canonist collections made north of the Alps.

It is difficult to overrate the significance of the rediscovery of the Digest. Knowledge of the outlines of Roman law could readily be obtained from the Roman law of the Visigoths and from Justinian's Institutes and Code. As F. W. Maitland observed, however,

The Digest was the *only* book in which medieval students could obtain a knowl-edge of Roman law *at its best*. The Institutes are a slight text book. The Code is made up of detached ordinances. The Novels are not merely detached ordi-nances but are penned in a pompous, verbose style, likely to do as much harm as good . . . but for the Digest Roman law could never have reconquered the world . . . Men would never have become *enthusiastic* students of other books . . . the man who first teaches the Digest is the man who first teaches what the modern world has meant by Roman law . . . it was only in the Digest that men could get any notion of keen and exact legal argument, precise definition etc. (*Letters*, vol. II, ed. P. Zutshi, Selden Soc. supp. ser. II, 1995, nr 37)

The major secular law school in the eleventh century was that of Pavia, the capital of the Lombard kingdom. The jurists of Pavia were primarily concerned with Lombard law, as contained in the *Liber Papiensis*, a collection of the edicts of the Lombard kings before the Frankish conquest and of Frankish capitularies. In their exposition of this text, the jurists of Pavia were the first jurists to use the method of the gloss alongside the text. On matters of substance they formed two groups, the *antiqui* and the *moderni*. The former adhered to the traditional understanding of the Lombard texts, whereas the latter were characterised by their readiness to refer to Roman law as a general law to supplement and interpret the Lombard law. The modernist contribution is summed up in the *Expositio* to the *Liber Papiensis*, which appeared about 1070. It refers to the sources that had been available in Italy for some time, that is, Institutes, Code and *Epitome Juliani*, but it also contains nine extracts from the Digest.

The jurists of Pavia did not give particular attention to the Digest, because Roman law was not their prime concern. Their concern was the law of the Lombard kingdom and their aim was to ensure that judges and advocates in the Lombard courts were properly prepared. They recognised the value of Justinian's texts in inculcating a sense of legal reasoning but they did not study those texts for their own sake. They were interested less in the juristic arguments of the Digest than with what could be gleaned from the Roman sources about the nature and purpose of law in general. The *Expositio* shows that jurists were no longer satisfied simply with making summaries of texts. They now wanted to interpret them in depth. Where adherence to the letter of a text would lead to injustice, the *Expositio* stressed that its rationale, the *ratio legis*, must be identified and the text understood in the light of that *ratio*.

4 THE CIVIL LAW GLOSSATORS

The school of Pavia pointed the way to a new approach to the study of legal texts but the honour of producing the first expositors of Justinian's compilation belongs not to Pavia but to Bologna. The first law teacher at Bologna was said to be a *causidicus*, or consultant judge, called Pepo, in the last decades of the eleventh century. According to the English theologian Ralph Niger, writing a century later, his teaching was based on the texts of the Code and the Institutes, but he was apparently in a position to cite the Digest in his forensic arguments. For example, in 1076 the court of Beatrice, Marchioness of Tuscany, held at Marturi, had to deal with a dispute over the entitlement to a piece of land between a monastery, which claimed ownership by virtue of a prior grant, and a long-standing possessor. The latter relied on forty-year prescription to retain the land but the court was persuaded that the prescription had been interrupted, since there had been a *restitutio in integrum* in favour of the monastery, in accordance with Digest 4.5.26, cited by Pepo.

Whatever Pepo's claims to have taught Justinian's law, it was Irnerius who marked the separation between the science of law and the practice of law. He had been a teacher of grammar and began his study of the legal texts with explanations of difficult terms that they contained. Then he moved on to whole passages. His comments were originally in interlinear glosses, which gradually expanded into the margins of the text. Irnerius was thus the first of a line of doctors at Bologna, known, from their characteristic method of expounding the texts, as the glossators.

The new approach was marked by a debate on how law fits into the general scheme of knowledge. The traditional view, expressed by Isidore of Seville, was that, since law deals with human behaviour, it must be categorised under ethics. Now it was said that this was only true so far as the content of the rules was concerned. In so far as it concerns the interpretation of words in a text, law is part of logic. Logic embraced all three arts of that part of the traditional education known as the trivium, namely, grammar, dialectic and rhetoric. The scholastic techniques developed in these disciplines were exploited by the masters of Bologna. For them law was a higher study, only to be undertaken by those who had already mastered the arts of the trivium.

The glossators regarded Justinian's texts as sacred and ascribed to them almost biblical authority. They accepted without question Justinian's assurance that the texts contained no contradictions that could not be reconciled by one who tackled them with a subtle mind (*Constitutio Tanta*, 15) and they took it for granted that the compilation as a whole contained all that was necessary to answer any conceivable legal problem. The opening fragment of the Digest says that jurists are called priests and a succeeding fragment defines jurisprudence as 'the knowledge of things human and divine'. Does this mean, asked the glossators, that the jurist should study theology? The answer was no, since 'everything is found in the Corpus iuris'.

One of the main difficulties they faced was the appalling lack of coherence in the arrangement of the texts. The same matters were dealt with in the Institutes, Digest and Code, but without any order. The Bolognese glossators did not tamper with the order of the texts approved by Justinian. They supplied cross-references to all the texts which dealt with a particular topic, explaining differences and marshalling the arguments for and against a particular result. Their familiarity with the texts as a whole is indicated by the fact that they could cite every fragment in the Corpus iuris by its first words. No later generation of Roman law scholars has had a closer familiarity with the texts. They used all the techniques of dialectic to squeeze the correct meaning from a text. For them every text, indeed every separate clause in every text, having been approved by the Emperor Justinian, had equal authority.

Various types of legal literature developed out of the glosses on individual texts. Summaries of the content of particular titles of the Digest or Code evolved into *summae* of the content of a whole part of the Corpus iuris, especially the Code and the Institutes. An *apparatus* was a collection of glosses covering the material contained in a particular title in a fuller manner than in a *summa*. A particular favourite for this treatment was the last title of the Digest, 50.17, *de diversis regulis iuris antiqui*, which contained over two hundred 'rules', many in the form of general maxims. The glossators delighted in *distinctiones*, elaborate classifications with many divisions and sub-divisions, sometimes illustrated by diagrammatic tables. There were collections of opposing views on particular points (*dissensiones dominorum*) and collections of *quaestiones*, disputed points, with arguments for each view set out with its supporting texts and usually a *solutio*. Whatever the form, however, everything they wrote revolved around Justinian's texts in all their complex entirety. The glossators worked in an incremental way, each generation imposing a new layer on that laid down by its predecessors.

Irnerius was succeeded by the generation of the Four Doctors, of whom the most distinguished were Bulgarus and Martinus Gosia. Bulgarus was pre-eminent at Bologna, where he was known as 'the golden mouth'. Martinus favoured a more liberal approach. They differed over the kind of interpretation of the texts that would produce sensible and just results. Bulgarus assumed that Justinian's law was equitable and that the interpreter's function, in relation to any text, was to seek out the *ratio legis*, the purpose of the particular rule. In order to find this, other texts might be consulted, so long as they related to the same subject matter. For Martinus, on the other hand, that was not enough. The apparent meaning of a rule, when taken in isolation, could be modified by reference to equity. This was not merely a general idea of fairness (*equitas rudis*), but the equity which was to be gleaned from a consideration of the Corpus iuris as a whole (*equitas constituta*). In interpreting a particular text, therefore, one was not limited to a consideration of other texts dealing with the same topic but could take into account any text which seemed to throw light on the problem.

Bulgarus was succeeded as leader of the Bolognese school by his pupil Johannes Bassianus, who perfected the method of expounding the texts. In his view a proper treatment of a difficult text should have four stages. First, there should be a bare statement of the problem without any elaboration. Secondly, the teacher should cite contrary texts and the *solutiones* which had been suggested. Thirdly, the matter should be projected on to a wider plane by the citation of general propositions that were relevant to the case. Such propositions, Bassianus said, were popularly known as brocards. Finally, there should be a broad discussion of the problem, either immediately in class or in the evening, when more time was available. This method started from the individual text and broadened the discussion outwards, first to other relevant texts on the same matter and then to the law as a whole.

One of the aims of glossatorial scholarship was to discover the general principles, or brocards, inherent in the Corpus iuris. Some of them were already assembled in the last title of the Digest, dedicated to maxims. Others were detached from their original context and were used as part of an argument on any matter to which they could be made relevant. Their function in litigation was to establish a presumption in favour of the party relying on them, but their exact scope was undefined and frequently they could be met by a counter-proposition, which put forward an opposing view. Collections of brocards appear in the last quarter of the twelfth century. They always introduced strings of texts, which either supported or denied the proposition adopted by the brocard. Although apparently a civil law invention, they were taken up with enthusiasm by the canonists. They directed the busy lawyer quickly to the textual authorities, with which he could embellish his argument and impress the judge; often they were used to 'blind the judge with science'.

Bassianus's pupil Azo began the task of synthesising the detailed case discussions of the previous generations of glossators. His *summa* on the Code was to have enormous influence, so that it came to be regarded as indispensible for legal practice; the adage was 'who does not have Azo, should not go to court'. Finally, a century after Irnerius, between 1220 and 1240, the opinions of the whole school of civil law glossators were collected together by Azo's pupil, Accursius, in what became the standard *Glossa ordinaria* to Justinian's texts. It contains over 96,000 separate glosses, immediately superseded all earlier work and was always copied, and later printed, together with the original texts.

Without the help offered by Accursius's Gloss, it was thought, the texts could only offer partial guidance. For centuries, the Accursian Gloss was the basis of any doctrine which claimed to be derived from Roman law. The maxim came to be accepted that 'What the Gloss does not recognise, the Court does not recognise.' It is only in the last decades of the twentieth century that serious study of pre-Accursian writing has revealed the wealth of ideas produced by the generations between Irnerius and Accursius. The authority of the Gloss is the origin of the idea, still characteristic of the continental civil law, that authoritative academic comment on a legal text is itself an authentic source of law.

5 CIVIL LAW AND CANON LAW

Canon law was soon added to civil law as a subject of study at Bologna. It started with the disadvantage that, by contrast with the civil law, it lacked an authoritative body of texts, comparable to Justinian's corpus. There were various unofficial collections of material of different kinds, statements from the Bible, decisions of Church councils, opinions of Church Fathers, decisions (decretals) of Popes and fragments of Roman law. At first the civil lawyers regarded this disparate jumble with disdain, as unworthy of consideration as an autonomous discipline.

A dramatic change followed the publication by the monk Gratian, about 1140, of his *Concordantia discordantium canonum*, an authoritative collection, which sought to reconcile apparent contradictions. Unlike earlier compilers, Gratian provided explanations of the texts he had selected for inclusion in what came to be known as his *Decretum*. It superseded earlier canonist collections and was quickly accepted as an appropriate subject for glossatorial exegesis by canonists. Unlike the civil law, however, the texts of the canon law were continuously increasing with the promulgation of new papal decretals, which themselves had to be collected in new compilations.

The immediate reaction of orthodox civil lawyers to Gratian's achievement was negative. They continued to treat canon law as an inferior discipline to their own. In their view, Gratian was trying to do the impossible and was giving a spurious air of harmony to self-contradictory material. In their opinion, only the civil law provided all the techniques necessary for understanding any kind of law, including canon law. By the 1160s the civil lawyers had to recognise canon law as a parallel discipline to civil law, with parity of esteem, but they tended to keep their studies separate from canon law, even when the subject that they were discussing was covered by both systems, such as marriage or usury.

The civil law was a self-contained system, which had no need of supplementation from any other system. On the other hand, it was not applied exclusively in any court but only where the local law was lacking. Canon law, by contrast, was applied in the courts of the Church in all matters that appertained to ecclesiastical jurisdiction (the precise limits of the latter were much disputed and varied from country to country). For Gratian, canon law was a divine law, on a par with the law of the Gospel itself. It had to be admitted, however, that canon law did not have the answers to all legal questions, as the civil law claimed to do. The *Decretum* itself stated that in matters left undefined by the canons, the civil law should be followed (D.10 p.c.6). How this applied in practice was a matter of keen debate among the early canonists, known as decretists.

The question of filling gaps in the canon law from the civil law was tied up with two wider issues, that of the legislative power of the Pope, as having equal authority with that of the emperor, and that of the nature of the proceedings in ecclesiastical courts. Should they anticipate the judgment of God, by applying moral rules in the tradition of the Penitentials, or were they public proceedings which had to follow similar rules to those of other public courts? Some canonists, such as the Frenchman Stephen of Tournai, held that civil law applied wherever it was not contrary to canon law. Others were less deferential to the authority of the civil law. In this formative period of their law, however, all canonists paid close attention to the debates among their senior partners, the civil law glossators.

At the beginning of the thirteenth century the decretists made a conscious effort to elucidate the precise legal effect of the canons by making comparisons with Roman law. This applied even in the sacramental parts of the canon law. For example, Laurentius Hispanus in his *Glossa Palatina* to the *Decretum* discusses the question whether a heretic can administer a valid baptism. He cites Inst. 2.8.1 to the effect that a non-owner can sometimes transfer ownership, as when he sells a security given to him by a debtor and the debt has not been paid. Similarly, argues Laurentius, a heretic can confer spiritual grace, even though he lacks that grace himself (*ad De consecratione*. D.4 c.23 *v.* Romanus).

Between 1188 and 1226, five compilations of papal decretals appeared. Then, in 1234, Pope Gregory IX promulgated a large collection of extracts from papal decretals, based partly on these older compilations. The work was edited by the Spanish Dominican Raymond of

Peñaforte, and was known as the *Liber extra* because it was outside (*extra*) Gratian's *Decretum*. It contains 1,971 chapters, arranged in five books. The order of treatment was cited by students according to the mnemonic verse 'judex, judicium, clerus, connubia, crimen', that is, judges and their powers, legal proceedings, clerical matters, marriages and crime. The Decretals were intended to form, with the *Decretum*, the law of the universal church. In 1298 a further collection appeared, promulgated by Boniface VIII and known as *Liber sextus*, since it supplemented the five books of the *Liber extra*.

The earlier compilations had concluded with a title containing general legal maxims, in imitation of the concluding title of Justinian's Digest. But where Justinian found 202 examples, Gregory's *Liber extra* only included eleven. The popularity of maxims and brocards increased in the thirteenth century and the *Liber sextus* concludes with a title of eighty-eight. Many were transferred from the corresponding title of the Digest (50.17), in some cases with the wording made more pithy. Some were abstracted from other parts of the Corpus iuris and, removed from their original context, acquired greatly extended meaning.

Thus a famous principle, much bandied about in political debate, is *quod omnes tangit debet ab omnibus approbari* ('what touches all should be approved by all'), which is *reg.*29 in the *Liber sextus*. Originally this statement was part of a ruling in which Justinian explains that, where there were several guardians of the same ward, their joint administration of the ward's property could not be ended without the consent of all (C.5.59.5.2). The canonists saw nothing strange about transferring the maxim from a private law context first to procedure and then to public law. Its authority came from the fact that it appeared somewhere in the texts of Justinian's law.

Certain other additions were made to the texts of authoritative canon law and by the end of the fourteenth century the Church had what came to be known as the Corpus iuris canonici, a compilation on a scale worthy of standing next to the Corpus iuris civilis of Justinian.

The compendious expression *utrumque ius*, 'both laws', was used as a qualification for those who had studied both systems. It also indicated a relationship between them that became increasingly close as time went on. By the thirteenth century the two systems were on an equal footing and the civil lawyers sought to keep them in distinct spheres. The civil law was concerned with the common good of man on earth and the canon law with keeping him from sin and ensuring the salvation of his immortal soul. Accursius (*gl. conferens generi ad Auth. Coll.*1.6, *quomodo oportet* *episcopos*) states that the Pope should not meddle with temporal matters nor the emperor with spiritual matters.

As later civil lawyers pointed out with exasperation, however, by reason of its concern with sin the Church usurped to itself jurisdiction over everything. From the time of the *Liber extra*, canon law covered many matters which were treated in Justinian's law. It included a large part of criminal law, from adultery and perjury to forgery and homicide; it touched private law at many points where a party might be tempted to sin, such as loan, the taking of interest, sale and real and personal security for debt. Because marriage was a sacrament, it was regulated by canon law and, as a result, all questions of family status fell within its purview.

Already in the twelfth century, problems arose in connection with the computation of degrees of blood relationship. This was crucial in ascertaining whether the parties to an apparent marriage were within the prohibited degrees of kinship. Civil law counted the degrees merely upwards from the parties to the common ancestor, whereas canon law counted them from one party up to the common ancestor and then down to the other party. As a result, many more cousins found that, under canon law, they were within the prohibited degrees, and so needed papal dispensations to marry, than would have been the case under civil law. The Fourth Lateran Council limited the prohibited degrees to four.

The glossators had tended to ignore such differences, but by the fourteenth century the two laws came to be dealt with together, even by civilian commentators. Many canonists were laymen and a qualification in both laws (*in utroque iure*) became quite common. The phrase 'both laws' began to refer to two aspects of what in many respects was regarded as a single system, a *ius commune* for the whole of Europe.

6 THE ATTRACTION OF THE BOLOGNA *STUDIUM*

By the end of the twelfth century the position of Bologna as the legal centre (or 'mother of laws') of Europe was unchallenged and the *studium* had thousands of law students from all over Europe. They were grouped in 'nations' according to their country of origin. For the first time since the fall of Rome, law in the West was an autonomous discipline, whose special techniques had to be learned over several years of rigorous study, at the conclusion of which a professional qualification was received.

The law students not only attended lectures. They cut their teeth as lawyers by participating in disputations on set topics, in which each side presented an argument with supporting texts, after which the master presiding gave his solution to the problem. They were expected to equip themselves with a personal set of the more important texts. Authorised booksellers, known as *stationarii exempla tenentes*, held certified copies of the texts, which they hired out to students so that they could make their own copies. When their period of study was over, they would have the basic material to take with them. In this way former students were able to disseminate a knowledge of what they had learned in their own countries.

Although the emphasis of the Bologna law school was academic rather than practical, the students who flocked there were not all motivated by a disinterested love of learning. The Gregorian reforms had stimulated many disputes of a quite unprecedented character. They could not be settled by sheer force, as had been the case in earlier centuries. There was a yearning for power to be legitimated, but standard collections of laws, whether of Roman or Germanic origin, offered little guidance on fundamental questions of jurisdiction and the like. Bishops and secular princes alike looked for men who could deploy arguments, based on principles which were objective and rational and had a universal authority. Only the Roman texts could provide such principles. The new legal learning provided its students with qualifications which won them positions of responsibility both in episcopal and princely establishments. Enlightened bishops sent their promising young chaplains to Bologna to acquire at least some knowledge of the new learning, while princes and nobles seeking to legitimate their power sought to ensure that its results were also available to them.

The University of Bologna was not founded by a deliberate act. It emerged out of the need, felt by the students of law, to organise themselves for the purpose of ensuring that they received the most effective teaching and obtained a recognised qualification. In contrast with the other twelfth-century universities of Paris and Oxford, established and governed by masters, Bologna became the model of a university governed by students, who employed the professors to teach them. Although other higher subjects, such as theology and medicine, were also taught there, law, both civil and canon, remained dominant.

Both the imperial and the papal authorities endeavoured to find favour with the Bolognese *studium*, by supporting it in its dealings with the municipal authorities of the city. The influx of students had created serious problems for the citizens but they did not want to lose the economic advantages that the students' presence brought them. The young

Emperor Frederick Barbarossa, on his way to Rome for his coronation in 1155, stopped at Bologna to meet the leading doctors of law and to seek their support, in justifying certain laws that he wished to enact. Having obtained their assistance, he promulgated the *Constitutio habita*, in which he conferred privileges on law students coming to Bologna, whom he described as 'pilgrims for the sake of study'. In particular Frederick recognised corporations of students, who were to be allowed to govern themselves in the manner of craft guilds. This concession enabled the students to negotiate with the professors but it also gave the *studium* as a whole a certain independence from the commune of Bologna.

By the beginning of the thirteenth century, the students were sufficiently strong that they could often get their way by threatening to secede from the town. The commune reacted by trying to keep them and it was now the turn of the papal authorities to intervene on the students' behalf. In 1217 Pope Honorius III pointed out that, instead of trying to compel the students to stay, it would be better for the commune to adopt measures that would encourage them to remain there of their own free will. Two years later, the Pope granted the archdeacon of Bologna the power to confer on successful students the right of teaching everywhere, thus indirectly subordinating the university to the Church.

The success of Bologna ensured its imitation through the foundation of law schools in other parts of Italy. There was a law school at Modena in 1175. The *studium* at Padua was begun in 1222, and the example was followed by other Italian centres, such as Pavia, where the old school of Lombard law developed into a school of civil and canon law. In 1224 the Emperor Frederick II founded the university of Naples, largely for the study of Roman civil law, and sought to ensure its success by commanding his subjects to study there rather than in Bologna. At first the order applied only to those in the kingdom of Sicily, but, in the course of his dispute with the Lombard League, to which Bologna adhered, he extended the ban on studying at Bologna to his subjects in his Lombard dominions and to those in Germany and Burgundy. This might have proved disastrous for Bologna but again Pope Honorius III stepped in and obtained a revocation of the ban.

7 THE NEW LEARNING OUTSIDE ITALY

Already in the early twelfth century there is evidence of the acceptance of the new Bolognese learning across the Alps in south-west France. This area, Provence in its wider medieval meaning, including Languedoc and the Dauphiné, was fertile ground for such influence. The regional customs contained more Roman elements, derived from the Visigothic and Burgundian collections of Roman law, than the customs of other regions. Already in the years 1127 to 1130, a law school in the diocese of Die in the Rhône valley, associated with the Augustinian canons of St Rufus, produced a summa on the Institutes, entitled *Iustiniani est in hoc opere*. Although the author did not know all parts of the Corpus iuris, he cited the *Digestum vetus*. More significantly still, he was familiar with the teaching of Martinus, still a young man, with whom he must have studied.

The *summa* on the Institutes is the earliest of a group of civil law works produced in Provence, such as the *Exceptiones Petri* and its related collections, known as the Tübingen and Ashburnham Law-Books (the designations refer to the locations of the manuscripts). Unlike the Bolognese works, whose authors are identified, the authors of these works are mostly anonymous. The Provençal writings are further distinguished from those produced at Bologna by being selective in the material taken from the Corpus iuris and by their attempts to organise that material under headings, sometimes loosely related to the order of the Institutes, rather than adhere to the arrangement of Code and Digest in the Bolognese manner. These works were at one time considered by scholars to be of Italian origin but from a pre-Bolognese period. Now they are recognised as the products of jurists who were influenced by Bolognese scholarship but felt free to abandon the latter's casuistic concentration on textual detail. Another genre of legal literature associated with the area is the *summa* of the Code, of which an early example is the *Summa trecensis*, compiled by a certain Gerard. A further work of the same type is *Lo codi*, which broke away from the universal use of Latin by being written in the Provençal language.

The reputation of the Rhone valley school extended outside Provence and it is significant that the Englishman Nicholas Breakspear, the future Pope Adrian IV, was attracted as a young man to study there. The Rhone valley school also attracted civil lawyers with an international reputation, such as the glossator Rogerius, who had studied and taught at Bologna. His main work is an unfinished *summa* of the Code, which shows the influence of the *Summa trecensis* and of *Lo codi*. He is also probably the author of a dialogue, *Enodationes quaestionum super Codice*, in which the author and Jurisprudentia discuss the nature of law and its interpretation in a colourful and imaginative way. Rogerius's unfinished *summa* was completed by the glossator Placentinus, an outspoken and somewhat arrogant man, who was forced to leave Bologna in the 1160s. He moved the teaching of civil law from Provence westwards to Montpellier, where he established a school. Placentinus taught there successfully, and produced his own *summae*, both of the Code and of the Institutes. After his death in 1192, teaching of civil law at Montpellier ceased but was revived a quarter of a century later.

Meanwhile the march of the new Roman law was continuing. At the end of the century, it is attested in Catalonia. Petrus de Cadorna, who went on to become a cardinal, was the first Catalan known to have acquired a purely civil law training and he was able to supply Latin translations of two Greek constitutions in the Code (C.3.10.1 and 2). Already in the 1160s an apparatus to the Institutes, probably written by Albericus, a minor Bolognese glossator, was produced at Rheims. Civil law was also taught in schools founded at Toulouse and Orleans. At Paris civil law acquired such popularity that there were general complaints that theology was being neglected in favour of an essentially secular study. In 1219 Pope Honorius III, in the bull *Super speculam*, prohibited the teaching of civil law in Paris, although he allowed the teaching of canon law to continue there.

In England, teaching of the new legal learning is associated with the Lombard Vacarius, who was recruited from Bologna in the 1140s by Archbishop Theobald of Canterbury specifically to assist him in the 'unheard-of disputes', in which he was engaged, particularly with the papal legate. Vacarius might have done some informal teaching in the cathedral school at Canterbury but his formal teaching began not, as was until recently thought, around 1150 in Oxford, but in the 1170s and further north. After arrival in England he was ordained and at some point moved to the northern province of York, where he acted as legal advisor to the archbishop of York. His personal teaching was probably in the cathedral school at Lincoln.

For the benefit of his students who could not afford the full civil law texts, Vacarius compiled a collection of essential texts taken from Digest and Code, including the *Tres libri*. It was arranged in nine books, in imitation of the (medieval) Code, and was called the Book of the Poor (*Liber pauperum*). In the 1190s this book was used as a textbook at Oxford, where the civil law was taught together with canon law. The students, known as *pauperistae*, gained a reputation for their arrogant assumption of superiority, despite a somewhat superficial knowledge of the civil law. Vacarius had serious pupils, however, who kept in touch with developments in Bologna and who formed a school, whose ideas can be discovered in the glosses to the manuscripts of the *Liber pauperum*.

The civil lawyers at Bologna were generally laymen but most of those who studied the civil law outside Italy were churchmen, primarily concerned with the administration of justice in the church courts. This did not, however, mean that they treated the civil law superficially, for they felt that, without some study of the civil law, they would not properly understand the nature of law and the legal process.

As more universities were founded, it was accepted that law in a university setting meant the study not of the local customary law but of civil and canon law. They were the only forms of law which had the universal character expected of a university discipline. Indeed no European university offered instruction in the law of the land until the seventeenth century. As a result, in every European country a university-trained lawyer was necessarily a Roman lawyer. Such lawyers came to share a common legal culture, based on the same texts, expounded in the same language, Latin.

The demands made on the glossators included a clarification of the elements of a rational procedure for implementing the law, of the nature of legislative authority and of the relationship between local law and the imperial law. Although there were several sporadic texts in the Corpus iuris on all these subjects, none of them was treated there in a coherent and detailed manner. Political realities required the twelfth-century civil lawyers to give them special attention and their views on these subjects must now be considered.

8 APPLIED CIVIL LAW: LEGAL PROCEDURE

The importance of deriving a rational procedure from the available texts was recognised equally by civilists and canonists and they developed such a procedure as a joint venture. The canonists needed it for their courts but only the civil law could provide the authorities on which it could be based. The Romans themselves did not separate procedure from substantive law and the relevant texts were scattered over the whole Corpus iuris civilis. In the twelfth century the need for a general proce dure was pressing, as dissatisfaction with the traditional methods of proof, based on various forms of ordeal, was growing.

The generation of glossators which succeeded Irnerius took the first steps to tackle the problem. Bulgarus, one of the Four Doctors, wrote a work called *Excerpta legum*, with the aim of elucidating the mysteries of law (*archana iuris*) to his friend Cardinal Aimericus, chancellor of the Church from 1123 to 1141. He begins with the elements of a legal action, the participants, statements of claim and defence, evidence, judgments and appeals. Some earlier writers had suggested that, apart from the parties and the judge, the advocates and the witnesses should also be considered as participants. But, said Bulgarus, the essence of a legal action is a proceeding of three persons, the plaintiff asserting his claim, the defendant denying it and the judge in the middle, discovering. Bulgarus explains that normally the burden of proof in a civil action is on the plaintiff and discusses how, in some cases where proof is lacking, the matter may be settled by oath.

Bulgarus's pupil Johannes Bassianus gave the impetus to a new genre of legal literature, the *ordo iudiciorum*, which sought to clarify what a civil action was, how it was begun and ended and how it could be avoided. Bassianus gave practical examples of how to draft a *libellus*, a statement of claim. Later writers looked for the principles underlying such a procedure, such as that the judges should decide cases according to the pleas of the parties, the *allegationes*, and not from their personal beliefs.

The elaboration of a rational procedure from the materials of Roman law was not just an academic exercise. Legally minded popes, such as Alexander III, required churchmen who decided disputes involving ecclesiastical bodies to follow the rules of the *ordo*, as the only means of ensuring that litigants' interests would be protected. The end of the twelfth century saw a flowering of procedural *ordines*, especially in the Anglo-Norman kingdom. At first they consisted exclusively of Roman material, culled mainly from the Code. They typically dealt with summons of the defendant, the giving of security for the parties' appearance, proctors who represented the parties, oaths, the effect of overclaim, defences, witnesses, compromises, the distinction between judges and arbitrators, judgments and appeals. Towards the end of the century, as the canonist authorities increased through the promulgation of more and more papal decretals, these procedural works became less dependent on civil law. They were intended for practitioners in both systems and the resulting procedure is properly designated Romano-canonical.

The procedural works culminated in the *Speculum judiciale* (Mirror of Justice) of Guglielmus Durandus, which appeared in 1271. Durandus was a Provençal, who studied canon law at Bologna and became a papal auditor, or judge dealing with appeals to Rome from all over the Christian world, and eventually a bishop in his native Provence. The *Speculum* relied heavily on earlier work, but Durandus wove it all together in a form that made it easy to consult. In four books he dealt with the persons involved in a legal action, civil procedure, criminal procedure and precedents of pleading, the latter part including precedents for deeds. The work ensured lasting fame for its author, often referred to as the Speculator.

In practice the Romano-canonical procedure, ultimately derived from the late-Roman professional procedure, was developed in the Church courts and in arbitrations conducted by churchmen. By the thirteenth century it was ready to be used in secular courts. The Parlement de Paris adopted a version of it which served as a model for other French courts. It was an entirely professional procedure, the judges personally investigating, in private, the facts which were not admitted by both sides. To ensure that the examining judge asked relevant questions, the parties suggested questions in advance, together with their initial statements of claim and defence. The evidence collected was all recorded in writing. Eventually an entirely written procedure was created, which, as it became more technical, needed professional advocates to operate it. If they were university trained, it was natural that they would cite the civil law that they had learned, where it advanced their argument. The adoption of the learned procedure was thus the first step to adopting parts of the civil law.

9 APPLIED CIVIL LAW: LEGISLATIVE POWER

The Digest and Code both assert the emperor's absolute power to legislate. 'What has pleased the prince has the force of law', states D.1.4.1. The original context of this remark, by Ulpian, was probably a reference to the emperor's power to settle a juristic dispute, in which differing views of the law had been put forward. In the Digest, however, it stood as a stark assertion of the emperor's absolute power. Another text referred to the emperor as 'freed from the bonds of the law' (D.1.3.1), that is, apparently above the law. In D.1.14.1, Ulpian explains the emperor's power to legislate as the result of the practice of the Roman people in formally conferring on each emperor, at the beginning of his reign, the power to do everything that was necessary for the benefit of the state (the so-called *lex de imperio* or *lex Regia*).

On the other hand, the text of Julian (D.1.3.32) on custom, to which we have referred (chapter 2, section 10), affirmed that legislation, like custom, derives its authority from popular consent. The idea that in some sense the emperor was the delegate of the people had support from

C.1.14.4 (*Digna vox*), a constitution of Theodosius II from 429, which states that the emperor should declare himself bound by the laws, since his authority depends on the laws and it is a mark of imperial authority to submit to the laws.

According to tradition, in the middle of the twelfth century the Emperor Frederick Barbarossa and his son Henry VI both consulted the leading civil lawyers on their powers. Frederick asked Bulgarus and Martinus whether in law he was lord of the world (*dominus mundi*). Bulgarus replied that in regard to private property he was not lord, but Martinus said that he was indeed lord of the world. (Martinus received Frederick's horse as a reward for his opinion, while Bulgarus got nothing.) Henry VI raised a similar question when he asked two of the Bolognese doctors, Lothair and Azo, to whom the supreme authority, *imperium*, belonged. Was it the emperor's alone or did other magistrates enjoy it as well? Lothair gave the answer the emperor wanted: the emperor, as *imperator*, alone has *imperium*. But Azo argued, on the basis of the texts, that a function of *imperium* is *iurisdictio*, 'the power of stating what is lawful'. The fullest *iurisdictio* belongs to the emperor alone but any magistrate in a city possesses it and so can lay down the law. Therefore, he concluded, *imperium* belongs to these other office holders as well.

When Azo investigated the source of the *iurisdictio* of the higher magistrates, he found it in the consent of the whole community considered as a collectivity (*universitas*). If the emperor's power came from the people through the *lex Regia*, popular consent must be the source of all legitimate authority. Earlier glossators had admitted this but argued that once the people had transferred legislative power to the emperor, they could not revoke it. Azo drew a distinction between the people as a group of individuals and as a community. The people as a group of individuals was excluded from legislative power by the *lex Regia*, but the people considered as a *universitas* retained legislative power. Azo's conclusion was momentous for political theory: the emperor has greater power than any individual but not than the people as a whole. In this way Azo was able to justify the *de facto* independence of the Italian city-states from the emperor. He could also argue that within his kingdom a king held the same power as the emperor.

Justinian's texts could thus provide support for various views on the source of legislative power. Great efforts were made to reconcile the notion that the prince was freed from the laws with the notion of *Digna vox* that the prince's power was limited. Increasingly rulers' advisors turned to those texts which emphasised the unrestricted power of the prince to govern and to legislate for the common good, as he saw fit. The civil law was thus placed in opposition to the feudal idea that viewed the relationship of the prince and his vassals as a kind of bargain in which the ruler's powers were balanced by his duties. It is this notion of kingship which seems to survive in Bracton's statement in the thirteenth century that in England the king was under God and the law, because the law makes the king.

10 CIVIL LAW AND CUSTOM

We have noted that those who were primarily concerned with the canon law of the Church courts normally prepared themselves with some study of the civil law, which was increasingly seen as a universal law. Within the boundaries of the Holy Roman Empire, reference to Roman law could be explained on the ground that it was imperial law, but more and more it was justified not for its formal authority but for its technical superiority over any possible rival. Unlike the canon law, however, no court applied just Roman law. The Church courts applied canon law to such matters as marriage and personal status; the courts of feudal lords applied feudal law to questions of landholding; the traditional community courts applied the local customary law to claims for compensation for wrongdoing. What the civil law supplied was a conceptual framework, a set of principles of interpretation that constituted a kind of universal grammar of law, to which recourse could be made whenever it was needed. Feudal or local courts sought in the first place to apply their own law but if that failed to provide a satisfactory solution for the problem in hand, they turned increasingly to the civil law. Thus when enforcement of customary law became an issue, Roman legal actions were adapted to enforce claims based on customary law.

Even the feudal law could be accommodated within the broad framework of the civil law. In the first half of the twelfth century Lombard scholars made a collection of feudal customs, the *Libri feudorum*, introduced by a Milanese judge called Obertus, which soon gained general acceptance as a convenient statement of the rules governing the relationship of lord and vassal. Towards the end of the century the civil lawyers calmly incorporated the *Libri feudorum* into the *volumen parvum*, or fifth volume of the Corpus iuris, together with the Institutes, the *Tres libri* and the *Authenticum* in nine *Collationes*. The *Libri feudorum* were added as a tenth *Collatio*. Probably the civil lawyers were motivated by a desire to prevent the lucrative work arising out of feudal disputes from falling into the hands of their rivals, the canonists.

They still had to accommodate the realities of the feudal relationship with the Roman law of property, which held that ownership (*dominium*) was indivisible. They noted some similarity between the feudal vassal and the Roman *emphyteuta*, or long lease-holder. Noting that the latter had a special version of the owner's action, called *vindicatio utilis*, while the owner had a *vindicatio directa*, they inferred that these actions corresponded to two different kinds of ownership: the feudal vassal had *dominium utile*, while the lord had *dominium directum*.

An important problem for all medieval jurists concerned the validity of a local custom which appeared to contradict the imperial law of the Corpus iuris. Despite Justinian's assurances to the contrary, the texts did not speak with one voice on this point. On the one hand, there was the Digest text of Julian (1.3.32), which affirmed that both custom and written law were based on popular acceptance and so custom could abrogate a prior law. On the other hand, there was the Code text (8.52.2), giving Constantine's rule that the authority of custom does not extend to the point where it contradicts either reason or a *lex*.

The glossators debated the problem fiercely. Irnerius held that Julian's text referred to a time when the people still enjoyed the power to lay down the law and so could abrogate legislation by tacit consent. In his own time, however, such power had been transferred to the emperor and the people could no longer by their practice affect the validity of imperial law. Irnerius's pupil, Bulgarus, distinguished between a general custom and a local custom. The former must always prevail over an earlier law, whether customary or written. The latter could abrogate the earlier law only if it was introduced with knowledge of its existence, and then only within the bounds of the locality. Bulgarus's rival Martinus disagreed. In his view, a custom can only affect an earlier custom; it can have no effect on a written law contained in the Corpus iuris. Bulgarus's successor at Bologna, Johannes Bassianus, went further than his master. The people know what they are doing when they introduce a custom. Therefore, so long as it is based on reason (as required by the Code text), a custom is valid, whether or not the people are aware of the prior law. Both written law and custom derive their authority from the will of the people. A law acquires no authority from the fact that it is in writing.

The Accursian Gloss gives the views of Bulgarus and Martinus but does not decide between them. In southern France, where Martinus's influence was strong, the general view was that the imperial law must prevail over custom. In England, on the other hand, doctrine moved strongly in the opposite direction. The local situation provided the context.

In the second half of the twelfth century, King Henry II imposed a central government over the whole of England. One of its expressions was the introduction of a royal court, which could deal with cases arising in every part of the country and from all sections of the people, Norman or Saxon. It was too early to adopt the Romano-canonical procedure, which was still in its infancy. Every action was started by a writ issued by the royal Chancery, at the request of the plaintiff. It ordered the king's representative in the area to bring the defendant named in the writ to answer the plaintiff's claim before the king's judges. The writ specified the circumstances which, if proved, would entitle the plaintiff to a verdict in his favour. The royal judges would decide precisely how the facts, as asserted by the parties, fitted with the terms of the writ and then the case was sent to a lay jury of twelve men from the locality, who heard the evidence in public and gave the verdict. In the requirement that every legal action should begin with a writ, provided by a state official, who could therefore control the type of matters that were brought to the king's court, and end with the decision of a lay tribunal on the facts of the case, the procedure of the courts of common law recalls the formulary procedure of classical Roman law. There was no direct influence but the parallel is striking.

The decisions of the royal judges on the effect of the various writs were said to be based on custom. Unlike the local customs applied in the local courts, which were derived from actual practice, however, the custom of the common law courts was largely elaborated by the judges themselves. It had to be discovered in the records of the courts. The glosses on custom to Vacarius's *Liber pauperum* go further than any continental gloss in supporting the validity of custom and thus give a theoretical foundation to the new customary common law, developed by the king's court.

Customary practice was strong in all aspects of law, even in the canon law. Although papal decretals were normally expressed in language which suggested that they were to be applied consistently throughout the Church, they were in practice often modified by local usage in the different ecclesiastical provinces. That this practice could be legitimated in the doctrine of Roman civil law was important for all lawyers.

11 CIVIL LAW AND LOCAL LAWS IN THE
THIRTEENTH CENTURY

The thirteenth century saw attempts in several European countries to set down the local law in writing and in every case those responsible turned to the civil law to provide organising categories and organising principles. The English common law was set out in the Latin treatise on the laws and customs of England, known as Bracton. Its core was written in the 1230s and it was later revised. Although based on the records of the royal court, it used, and sometimes adapted, the categories of Roman civil law, derived from Azo's *Summa Codicis*. The author of Bracton understood that if the laws of the king's court were to be set out in a manner approaching coherence, he would need a structure of general notions, which were articulated only in Roman law. Many passages echo the language of Digest and Code, not by formal citation but by the use of phrases from the Roman texts, which the author has woven into his exposition. They show that he had made Roman law part of his way of thinking as a lawyer. His treatise equipped the nascent common law with the minimum theoretical structure that it needed to grow in a coherent way.

When kings wanted to legislate, they turned to civil lawyers for help. Edward I, king of England from 1272 to 1307 (and lord of substantial parts of France), was very interested in problems of government and law and was responsible for several pieces of legislation that earned him the (exaggerated) title of 'the English Justinian'. For this work he specially recruited Francis Accursius, son of the great glossator, and a well-known civil lawyer in his own right, into his service.

At the same time as Bracton was compiling his collection of English law, the Emperor Frederick II in 1231 promulgated a collection of laws for his Sicilian kingdom, known as the *Liber Augustalis* or Constitutions of Melfi. In substantive content these laws are not obviously Roman, but Roman texts were used to justify the law-making power of the emperor and the procedure to be adopted in the royal courts. Again the underlying assumption seems to have been that, without a clothing of Roman law, the laws of the kingdom, even when promulgated by the emperor, would not appear to be fully authentic. Gradually the Roman civil law was permeating all legal culture; it provided the categories, the methods of legal reasoning and the forms of argumentation, which were essential for anyone who wished to be considered a jurist.

The *Constitutio puritatem* laid down the duties of Frederick's judges in the face of a multiplicity of overlapping laws. In the first place they must apply royal legislation. If there is no relevant rule to be found there, local customs may be applied, so long as they are good customs; in the absence of a rule in legislation or approved customary law, the judges should turn to the *ius commune*, which is explained as Lombard law and Roman law. Lombard law was the only Germanic law to have been the subject of scholarly interpretation (at Pavia). Henceforth, however, no law was taught in law schools but civil and canon law. Even Frederick's royal constitutions had no place in the curriculum of the law school at Naples, which he founded.

In Spain the legal situation was much affected by the Moorish domination. The *Liber iudiciorum*, a seventh-century collection, based on earlier collections of Visigothic and Roman laws, which had originally been applied to the Visigothic and subject populations but had become territorial, provided some basis for the regional customs. The Moorish occupation, beginning early in the eighth century, covered the whole peninsula, except for the far north and Catalonia, until the end of the tenth century. The Reconquista proceeded during the eleventh and twelfth centuries and by 1200 the northern two-thirds of the country had been freed from Moorish domination. It was, however, not united, since, as different parts were freed, they became independent kingdoms, each with its own set of customs, set out in a multitude of written 'fueros'.

The leading kingdom was Castile and Leon. The earliest Spanish university was established in the first decade of the thirteenth century at Palencia and moved in 1239 to Salamanca, which became a centre for civil and canon law. In the middle of the thirteenth century, two remarkable kings, Ferdinand III and Alfonso X, were able to exploit the new learning in order to counter the diversity of laws in their dominions. In the style of Frederick II in Sicily, they sought to introduce a modern system that would act as a unifying force and bring Castile into the mainstream of European legal thought.

Ferdinand initiated an ambitious set of law books, culminating in the *Siete partidas*, published by Alfonso, known as 'the wise'. The division into seven parts glowed with religious significance and may have been modelled on the sevenfold division which Justinian imposed on the Digest for educational purposes (*Constitutio Tanta*, 1–8). Alfonso had been persuaded of the virtues of Roman law by his tutor, who had studied at Bologna, and personally led the team of compilers. The work they produced was a mixture of traditional customs of Castile and Leon, of civil and canon law and of rules derived from the Old and New Testaments and from patristic writers. Although by inclination favouring Roman law, Alfonso had to make it acceptable to his subjects.

The *Siete partidas* were written in the vernacular rather than in Latin, and were comprehensive in scope, covering general notions of law and custom, procedure, property, marriage and marital property, contracts, succession on death and criminal law. Roman and canon law influences are noticeable in all parts. Alfonso was not strong enough to impose this legislation throughout his kingdoms. The nobility, whose privileges he had attempted to curtail, and the municipalities initially found it too foreign. Gradually, however, its merits were recognised and the more professionally trained the judges became, the more they turned to the *Siete partidas*.

Whether the recording of local law was achieved through legislation or was left to private individuals, the use of the civil law was the same. A well-known example from France is the treatise, written about 1280, by Philippe de Beaumanoir, bailli or judge of the Count of Clermont's court in Beauvaisis, on the Custom of Beauvaisis. He wrote in French, not Latin, and remained faithful to the customary law actually applied in his court. Yet he was clearly well trained in the civil law and, like Bracton, he adapted Roman law to quite unroman institutions, to give them greater authority. Thus he cites the maxim 'what pleases the prince has the force of law' to support the right of the king of France, when embarking on an expedition, to suspend the obligations of knights joining his army. One part deals with renunciations, clauses inserted into a charter in which a party renounced a possible appeal to some rule, usually by way of defence. Some of these, such as the complaint that the seller has received less than half the value of what he has sold (*laesio enormis*), are clearly of Roman origin and were probably copied from pleading formularies. The section on procedure shows the influence of the Romano-canonical works on procedure and the section on contracts, a subject that was not highly developed in local customs, drew considerably on Roman sources.

In the thirteenth century Roman civil law became, together with canon law and theology, part of a common Christian learned culture shared by those who occupied positions of authority, both lay and ecclesiastical. As such it was more readily exported east of the Rhineland into areas that were never part of the old Roman empire. For example, Anders Sunesen was a Dane of noble family who was sent to France, Italy and England to learn theology and law. On his return to Denmark he was made chancellor to the king, provost of Roskilde cathedral and from 1201 to 1224 Archbishop of Lund. He produced two works in Latin, designed to introduce the elements of the new learning to those of his fellow-countrymen who were literate. One, the *Hexaemeron*, was a statement in verse of Christian doctrine, as expounded by the Paris theologians. The other is a Latin version of the laws of Scania (at that time part of Denmark), in which he used Roman legal terms and so put the customary law into a Roman context. Sunesen's work indicates that the pace of cultural Europeanisation was quickening.

Despite the *de facto* validity of local law, Roman civil law provided an accepted 'mind-set', which formed the basis for political and legal thought throughout Europe. As part of the common culture of Christian Europe, it appeared quite naturally in great works of philosophy and literature. St Thomas Aquinas's *Summa theologica* and Dante's *Divina commedia* offer ready examples. For his philosophical principles, Aquinas draws on Aristotle, who for him is 'the philosopher'. For his examples of particular kinds of human behaviour and for some definitions, he draws on Roman law, and particularly Ulpian, who is 'the jurisconsult'. Aquinas's definition of justice as 'the constant and perpetual will to attribute to each his due' is that of Ulpian (D.1.1.10pr.).

Dante gives Justinian a prominent place as a sacred figure both in his *Paradiso*, books 6 and 7, and in his political works, where he identifies the Corpus iuris with Reason itself. Many passages from Dante, as from Aquinas, show how phrases from the texts of the Corpus iuris had become part of general educated discourse, even among non-lawyers.

12 THE SCHOOL OF ORLEANS

After the publication of the Accursian Gloss, the study of the civil law in Bologna, while still intense, lost some of its freshness and excitement. In the second half of the thirteenth century, the focus of study of Justinian's texts switched to Orleans, where civil law studies received a boost from the papal prohibition of its study in Paris. The earliest teaching there, in the 1240s, was by Italian scholars. The best known, Guido de Cumis, had had the temerity, when being examined by Accursius at Bologna, to question the correctness of one of his glosses and soon afterwards thought it prudent to leave for France.

The two teachers who gave Orleans its special character, Jacobus de Ravanis (Jacques de Revigny) and Petrus de Bellapertica (Pierre de Belleperche), both learned their law at Orleans. They did not introduce any particular novelty into the teaching of the civil law but extended certain tendencies which were already observable at Bologna, particularly the use of dialectical reasoning. Instead of the ingenious citation of texts, they adopted a freer approach, relying on logical argument and frequently extending the *ratio* of a text by analogy to what the Bolognese would have regarded as beyond the permissible limit. *Quaestiones de facto*, discussions of problems arising out of fact-situations (which might be hypothetical), were given an important place in the curriculum and some of these involved the effect of local customs. Both Jacobus and Petrus were clerics, who ended their careers as bishops. Yet they treated the civil law as quite distinct from the canon law. Their students, who were almost all clerics, made Orleans for a short period the Bologna of the north.

The Orleans masters expounded all parts of the Corpus iuris in detail, but since they scrupulously followed the original order of the texts they made no attempt to arrange their material systematically. The vehicle for transmitting their learning back to Italy was Cinus from Pistoia, a nobleman, poet and friend of Dante, who divided his career between public service and teaching. His main work was an exhaustive Commentary on the Code, which shows the influence of Jacobus de Ravanis. He introduced the latter's approach to Italy and in particular to his great pupil, Bartolus.

FURTHER READING

The standard reference works for medieval law and early modern law are F. Wieacker, trans. T. Weir, *A History of Private Law in Europe*, Oxford 1995; M. Bellomo, *The Common Legal Past of Europe, 1000–1800*, trans. L. Cochrane, Washington, D.C. 1995; O. F. Robinson, T. D. Fergus and W. M. Gordon, *An Introduction to European Legal History*, 2nd edn, London 1994; P. Vinogradoff, *Roman Law in Medieval Europe*, 2nd edn, Oxford 1929; *The Roman Law Tradition* (essays on selected topics), ed. A. D. E. Lewis and D. J. Ibbetson, Cambridge 1994; the various fascicules of *Ius Romanum Medii Aevi*, Milan from 1961; J. A. C. Smith, *Medieval Law Teachers and Writers, Civilist and Canonist*, Ottawa 1975; F. Calasso, *Medio Evo del Diritto*, 1, Milan 1954; H. Coing, *Handbuch der Quellen und Literatur der neueren europäischen Privatrechtsgeschichte*, Munich 1973; A. Padoa-Schioppa, *Il Diritto nella Storia d'Europa, Il medioevo*, 1, Padua 1995.

3.1. J. F. Winkler, 'Roman law in Anglo-Saxon England', *Journal of Legal History*, 13 (1992), 101.

3.2. For the Gregorian Reforms and legal development, H. Berman, *Law and Revolution: The Formation of the Western Legal Tradition*, Cambridge, Mass. 1983.

3.3. For Pavia, C. Radding, *The Origins of Medieval Jurisprudence, Pavia and Bologna 850–1150*, New Haven 1988, and review of A. Gouron, *TvR*, 57 (1989), 178.

3.4. S. Kuttner, 'The revival of jurisprudence', in *Renaissance and Renewal in the Twelfth Century*, ed. R. L. Benson and G. Constable, Oxford 1982, 301; P. Stein, Introduction to *The Teaching of Roman Law in England around 1200*, Selden Soc. supp. ser. 8, 1990; E. Cortese, *Il rinascimento giuridico medievale*, Rome 1992; W. P. Müller, 'The recovery of Justinian's Digest in the middle ages', *Bulletin of Medieval Canon Law*, NS 20 (1990), 1. On Pepo, L. Schmugge, 'Codicis Justiniani et Institutionum baiulus', *Ius Commune* 6 (1977), 1; B. Paradisi, 'Il giudizio di Martiri: alle origini del pensiero giuridico bolognese', *Rendiconti della Classe di Scienze Morali, Accademia dei Lincei*, series IX, vol. V (1994). For Bassianus's teaching, P. Weimar, 'Die legistische Literatur und die Methode des Rechtsunterrichts der Glossatorenzeit', *Ius Commune* 2 (1969), 47. P. Weimar, 'Argumenta Brocardica', *Studia Gratiana* 14 (Collectanea S. Kuttner IV), Bologna 1967, 89.

3.5. J. Brundage, *Medieval Canon Law*, London 1995; Gratian, *The Treatise on Laws* (Decretum DD.1–20), trans. A. Thompson, with the Ordinary Gloss, trans. J. Gordley, Washington, D.C. 1993; R. H. Helmholz, *The Spirit of Classical Canon Law*, Athens, Ga. 1996; on Larentius Hispanus, E. F. Vodola, 'Fides and culpa: the use of Roman law in ecclesiastical ideology', *Authority and Power: Studies for W. Ullmann*, ed. B. Tierney and P. Linehan, Cambridge 1980, 83.

3.6. A Garcia y Garcia, 'The faculties of law', in *A History of the University in Europe*, vol. I, ed. H. De Ridder-Symoens, Cambridge 1992, ch. 12; M. Bellomo, *Saggio sull' Universita nell'eta del diritto comune*, Catania 1979.

3.7. A. Gouron, *La science du droit dans le midi de la France au Moyen Age*, London 1984; P. Stein, 'The Vacarian School', *Journal of Legal History*, 13 (1992), 23.

3.8. L. Fowler-Magerl, *Ordo iudiciorum vel ordo iudiciarius*, Ius Commune Sonderhefte 19, Frankfurt 1984. J. P. Dawson, *A History of Lay Judges*, Cambridge, Mass. 1960, ch. 2; R. C. van Caenegem, Procedure (History), *International Encyclopedia of Comparative Law*, XVI, 2.

3.9. K. Pennnington, *The Prince and the Law, 1200–1600*, Berkeley, Calif. 1993; M. P. Gilmore, *Argument from Roman Law in Political Thought, 1200–1600*, Cambridge, Mass. 1941; *Cambridge History of Medieval Political Thought c. 350–c. 1450*, ed. J. H. Burns, Cambridge 1988.

3.10. P. Stein, 'The Civil Law doctrine of custom and the growth of case law', *Studi G. Gorla*, Milan 1994, 1.371; A. Gouron, 'Coutume contre loi chez les premiers glossateurs', *Renaissance du pouvoir legislatif et genèse de l'état*, ed. A. Gouron and A. Rigaudiere, Montpellier 1988, 117.

3.11. J. M. Powell, *The Liber augustalis or Constitutions of Melfi*, Syracuse, N.Y. 1971; E. N. van Kleffens, *Hispanic Law until the End of the Middle Ages*, Edinburgh 1968; E. Galto, J. Alejandre Garcia and J. M. Garcia Marin, *El derecho historico de los pueblos de Espana*, 3rd edn, Madrid 1982; for Anders Sunesen, R. Bartlett, *The Making of Europe: Conquest, Colonization and Cultural Change 950–1350*, London 1993, 289; J. M. Aubert, *Le droit romain dans l'oeuvre de Saint Thomas*, Paris 1955; F. Cancelli, 'Diritto romano in Dante', in *Enciclopedia Dantesca*, II. 472.

3.12. R. Feenstra, 'L'Ecole de droit d'Orleans au treizième siecle et son rayonnement dans l'Europe medievale', *Revue d'histoire des Facultés de droit et de la science juridique*, 13 (1992), 23.

CHAPTER 4

Roman law and the nation state

Bartolus, who gave his name to the school which dominated the study of
the civil law during the fourteenth and fifteenth centuries, was born in
1313 or 1314 in Sassoferrato, a small village in the Marches, and died in
1357. He began his studies of law, at the age of thirteen or fourteen, at
Perugia under Cinus and later went on to Bologna, where he took his
doctorate at the age of twenty. He was a judge in the small town of Todi
and then devoted himself to teaching, first at Pisa and then at Perugia,
where he died. His short life was completely absorbed by the law and his
output was phenomenal: apart from treatises on particular topics, he
wrote exhaustive commentaries on all parts of the Corpus iuris, which
in the early printed editions fill nine folio volumes.

True, much of the material consisted of citation of his predecessors
but Bartolus always added something of his own, usually a clear path
through the thickets of earlier debates, indicating a practical solution to
a problem. Under his influence the study of the civil law became less
purely academic and more orientated towards the legal problems of the
day. He and his followers continued to expound the texts in the form in
which they were transmitted but their aim was no longer to explain the
meaning of those texts as they stood. Rather they sought to find in them
rules which would be appropriate for late medieval society but would still
carry the authority of imperial law.

Bartolus realised that the law had to be accommodated to the facts.
On the question of the emperor's power over the Italian cities, he was
able to build on Azo's views. Although in law the emperor was lord of
the world, Bartolus observed that in practice many peoples did not obey
him. In the Italian city-states, the people recognised no superior, they
made laws as they chose and so, he concluded, they possessed *imperium*,

with as much power within their territories as the emperor had generally. If they had been exercising this power for a long time, they need not
prove any concession from the emperor. Indeed, when the people confer
power on their rulers, the latter are the delegates of the people, who
retain ultimate authority.

Bartolus's practical tendency can be illustrated from his approach to
the problems that arose where different laws came into conflict: between
civil law and local law, between one local law and another and between
civil law and canon law.

Bartolus confronted the issue of a conflict between civil law and local
law in a discussion of a custom of Venice. This custom accorded validity to a will if it had three witnesses, which was directly contradictory of
the Roman rule that required a minimum of five witnesses (C.6.23.31).
Bartolus sought the reason for holding a local custom to be void, if it
conflicted with imperial law, and concluded that it must be that it was
thereby presumed to be a bad custom. The Roman emperors, however,
are known to have allowed conflicting local customs to exist by way of
privilege. It follows that it must have been possible to rebut the presumption that a conflicting custom is necessarily a bad custom. Justinian's law
could only invalidate customs already in existence in his time. It is possible to prove that a later custom is good, even if it conflicts with
Justinian's law. The Venetians knew their own needs best. If they thought
it unreasonable to expect five merchants to interrupt their business activities in order to witness a will, a rule according validity to a will with only
three witnesses should be valid or else testators' last wishes would be frus-
trated. In this way Bartolus used Roman arguments to stand Justinian's
rule on its head.

Although Bartolus had to justify the existence of a particular law (*ius
proprium*) alongside the *ius commune*, he gained acceptance for the notion
that local statutes must be interpreted according to the methods established by the *ius commune* and in such a way as to derogate as little as possible from the *ius commune*. There are no rules in the Corpus iuris which
deal expressly with the conflict between different secular laws. In
Justinian's time almost all those living in the Roman empire were Roman
citizens, so that problems of conflict did not arise. In the complex world
of fourteenth-century Italian city-states, on the other hand, such problems were pressing and general rules were sorely needed. The glossators
had held that a person's law is that of the community of which he is a
citizen, but problems arose when two merchants from different cities
made a contract with each other.

Bartolus took specific cases reported in the Corpus iuris and general-ised their rulings, producing a coherent set of convenient rules, nowhere expressly stated in the Corpus iuris but claiming the authority of that law. The procedure in a civil action must always be governed by the law of the court in which the action is brought. As to the rules to be applied, however, the form of the contract must be governed by the law of the place where it was made, whereas any issue concerning the performance of the contract must be ruled by the law of the place where it should have been carried out.

The conflicts between civil law and canon law had to be dealt with by conciliatory methods. One problem, in which the two laws came into conflict, was that involving a will that the testator had confirmed by an oath, in which he swore not to change its terms in a subsequent will. The canonists considered the vital element to be the oath. For Durandus, for example, there was no problem. Every oath, which could be carried out without prejudice to one's immortal soul, had to be observed. The civil-ians emphasised the principle of freedom of testation. A testator must be free to change his mind and revoke the earlier will, by making a new will, at any time before he dies. The oath is not binding on him since, by purporting to limit this freedom, it is contrary to the law.

Later jurists, particularly the Orleans masters, made valiant efforts to reconcile the two positions, by allowing validity to a later will under certain conditions. The basic question was whether the law should allow an irrevocable will. Bartolus was determined that it should not but, unlike some of his predecessors, he could not just ignore canon law. In his view an attempt to deprive the testator of his freedom of testation was immoral (*contra bonos mores*) and as such was not binding, even by canon law. His conclusion was stated in the general rule that whatever is disapproved by the authority of the law is not validated by the force of an oath. Eventually Bartolus's accommodation of civil and canon law was accepted.

By making explicit the rationale that seemed to lie behind the spare rulings of the Roman texts, Bartolus was able to produce a set of new rules, which could claim to enjoy the authority of imperial law. Jurists were agreed that henceforth no one could be a lawyer who was not a Bartolist (*nemo jurista nisi Bartolista*). His methods were followed by a whole school, known as Commentators, of whom the most distinguished was his pupil Baldus de Ubaldis.

Baldus dominated the second half of the fourteenth century, dying in 1400. He commented not only in the civil law but also canon law and feudal law and perfected the opinion (*consilium*), a discussion of the legal issues raised by a particular case. This form of legal literature completed the adaptation of the civil law to contemporary problems.

By the fourteenth century the *ius commune* consolidated its position as part of a common Christian culture of Europe. It is this unity of culture which explains why law and religion were so closely related in late medieval writing. At times the intermingling of Roman law and theology produced a result that, to modern eyes accustomed to the separation of each discipline, seems bizarre. The spate of fourteenth-century popular tracts dealing with the trial of Satan provide an example. Their aim was twofold: first, to show that by the sacrifice of Christ hell had lost its power over mankind and that men could claim the atonement as a matter of justice as well as of grace, and secondly, to spread an understanding of the elements of legal procedure, by which justice was put into effect. One of these tracts, attributed (falsely) to Bartolus, was translated into German and is worth description as an example of the genre.

Satan appears before the court of Christ to bring an action against mankind. It is an *actio spolii* for depriving hell of its rightful possessions. The defendant fails to appear on the assigned day and Satan asks for judgment by default. Christ grants an adjournment on the ground of equity and by virtue of the judge's discretionary powers. The next day the Virgin Mary appears as an advocate for mankind. Satan objects to her, first, on the ground that she is a woman and unfit to be an advocate, and secondly, on the ground of her relationship with the judge. Christ overrules the objection. The Virgin argues that Satan is only entitled to possession in God's interest and Christ dismisses the *actio spolii*. Satan then seeks to bring a property action, claiming that he is entitled to mankind on the ground of man's original sin and God's words to Adam that he would die when he ate the forbidden fruit. The Virgin makes an exception (defence) that Satan himself was the cause of the fall of man and that no party is entitled to benefit from his own fraud. Satan makes a replication (reply to a defence) to the effect that, even if this were correct, mankind should be condemned by intervention of the judge (*officio iudicis*), since justice should not allow a crime to go unpunished. The Virgin protests that this amounts to an illegal change of plea by the plaintiff and produces her decisive argument, that Christ's voluntary suffering for mankind has satisfied justice. Satan's claims are therefore dismissed.

This treatment of a theological topic in terms of legal procedure seemed natural enough to an age that regarded theology and law as twin aspects of the same European Christian culture.

2 THE IMPACT OF HUMANISM

By the end of the fifteenth century the *ius commune* developed by the Bartolists was becoming more and more influential throughout Europe, as new universities were founded and more jurists were trained in the traditional learning. At the same time, however, the more it was adapted to find solutions to contemporary problems, the further the *ius commune* moved away from the law of Justinian, from which its authority derived. Its practitioners were self-sufficient and were convinced that the texts, Gloss and commentaries together contained all that was necessary for a complete understanding of the law. They wrote in medieval Latin and made no concessions to elegance or good style. They were thus ripe targets for exponents of the new learning of the Renaissance.

In the fifteenth century Italian scholars had become aware of the riches of classical antiquity in all its aspects. They seized on anything that threw light on ancient society and its thought and avidly studied texts which had lain dormant for centuries. The Roman law texts had been known and studied since the twelfth century, but its scholars had not been very interested in what they had to say about classical antiquity. A scholar who approached the texts of the Corpus iuris with the critical attitudes of the new humanism was bound to be disappointed, if he sought elucidation in the work of the glossators and Commentators. A humanist scholar was full of questions which they had not asked. He wanted to know about the authority of the text, how accurate it was, what were the fact-situations that lay behind the rulings of the classical jurists, but such matters had been almost ignored by previous exponents. So the humanist scholars found themselves wading through turgid discussions, written in barbarous medieval Latin, that threw little light on what they wanted to know.

The humanists at Pavia in northern Italy in the middle of the fifteenth century were shocked by the form in which they found the texts of the classical jurists, excerpted in the Digest. In their eyes, Tribonian, Justinian's minister in charge of the compilation, had not only excerpted the texts but in the process had mutilated them and introduced linguistic barbarisms. In his *Elegantiae linguae Latinae*, Lorenzo Valla praised the classical jurists and condemned not only Tribonian but also all the medieval commentators from Accursius to Bartolus for their bad Latin. Their insensitivity to correct language was proof, in Valla's view, that they could not be competent lawyers. Valla demonstrated that the so-called Donation of Constantine, a document by which the emperor was supposed to have granted temporal power to the Pope, and which had been accepted as genuine by most of the medieval exponents of civil and canon law, was a fake. His proof was partly based on the language of the Donation and partly on the anachronism that Constantine was supposed to have given the Bishop of Rome jurisdiction over the patriarch of Constantinople, who did not exist at the time. Thus humanism engendered a new critical attitude to the sources of law.

3 HUMANISM AND THE CIVIL LAW

The fifteenth-century Italian humanists were aware that the texts of the Digest, which were available to them, were faulty. The glossators and Commentators had been satisfied with the *litera bononiensis*, the traditional text which had been used at Bologna already in the eleventh century and which was the basis for the early printed editions of the Digest. The humanists recognised that the manuscript in the Laurentian Library in Florence (F) was older and closer to the original, but it was not easy to consult, as permission to see it was rarely granted.

The humanist Politian, although not a jurist, saw the need for a thorough study of F, which he believed to be the actual manuscript which Justinian had sent to Pope Vigilius in the 550s (as indeed is possible). He obtained permission from Lorenzo the Magnificent to make a collation of F with a printed edition. He worked intensively, noting at the end of the *Digestum vetus* that he finished collating it at 12.30 a.m. on 19 July 1490; six weeks later he completed the whole collation. Although Politian published only a few of his readings of F, he established the idea that the Florentine was the archetype of the Digest tradition and the best text was one based on it.

The first humanist jurists, who appeared in the first half of the sixteenth century, concentrated their efforts on ridding the texts of the glosses and commentaries that engulfed them. The Frenchman Guillaume Budé (Budaeus), in his *Annotationes in Pandectas* in 1508, although a jurist, showed more interest in the unusual words found in the Digest and in what it had to teach about ancient life than in the law itself. He described the commentaries, which showed no interest in such questions, as a malignant cancer on the texts, which had to be cut away. His German contemporary Ulrich Zäsi (Zasius), Clerk of the city council of Freiburg im Breisgau and professor in the university, called the commentaries a giant creeper which had taken root around the texts. Zasius was concerned about their legal meaning. As he expressed the new humanist approach in his *Lucubrationes* (1518), 'If the jurists had not always adhered so blindly to the authority of the Gloss and Bartolus, the true meaning of the law would now be seen more clearly and in greater purity, and most of the obnoxious commentaries, stuffed as they are with errors, would vanish. The only genuine interpreters are those who try to explain the sources themselves.' The emphasis was no longer on finding a workable rule for a contemporary problem but rather on revealing the original meaning of Justinian's texts.

The most influential jurist of this first phase of legal humanism was the Italian Andrea Alciato (Alciatus). He was thirty years younger than Zasius but published three short works, that made his name, in the same year as that of Zasius, 1518. It was the *Paradoxa* (which set out objections to received opinions) that had the biggest impact. Born in Milan, Alciatus studied law in Pavia under the last masters of the Bartolist methods, Jason de Mayno and Filippus Decius, but at the same time was caught by the excitement of humanist learning. He set himself the task of combining legal and humane studies, beginning with the reconstruction of Roman political institutions, not only from a purely historical standpoint but also from that of a jurist.

Alciatus taught at Avignon from 1518 to 1522 and introduced the new approach to law into France, where it was accepted with enthusiasm and became known as the *mos gallicus*, by contrast with the traditional Bartolist approach, now called the *mos italicus*. From 1529 Alciatus taught at Bourges, which became the main centre of legal humanism. Bourges was a Huguenot stronghold and almost all of the prominent French legal humanists were Protestant. Indeed the movement was seriously weakened after the Massacre of St Bartholomew in 1573, when many of its leading figures either fled from France or were killed. There is a clear parallel between their legal and their theological thinking. Just as the Church reformers were disputing the authority of the Church Fathers and proposing a return to the pure word of Holy Scripture, so the legal humanists wanted to revive the true law of Justinian, by appealing to the undiluted word of the texts.

The early legal humanists were concerned to improve the quality of their texts but, instead of following Politian's lead and systematically collating their texts with the Florentine manuscript, they relied largely on conjecture, using their knowledge of antiquity to guess what the text ought to be. It was not until 1553, almost sixty years after the death of Politian, that Lelio Torelli, in collaboration with the distinguished Spanish scholar Antonio Agustín, produced an edition of the Digest based on the Florentine manuscript.

The greatest humanist textual critic was Jacques Cujas (Cujacius). He recognised the importance of F, but realised that one could not slavishly follow the best manuscript reading; one had to take account of the legal conclusion to which that reading led and consider whether, in all the circumstances, the Roman jurist in question was likely to have written it. For Cujacius that meant balancing the reading of F against the *ratio iuris*, or principle behind the rule. To do that successfully required an encyclopedic knowledge both of the texts of the Corpus iuris and of humanist studies of ancient literature generally. Cujacius was unsurpassed in this regard and his works are still cited on the interpretation of Justinian's texts. He and his colleagues began the study of interpolations in the Digest texts.

In their task of recovering the true Roman law from the obfuscations of the glossators and Commentators, the humanists realised that Justinian's texts revealed not only the law of sixth-century Byzantium but also the law of the second and third centuries, the period of the great jurists whose works were excerpted in the Digest. This they identified as the classical period of Roman law. By careful detective work they could even reconstruct the law of the Twelve Tables of the early republic. Already in 1515 the Frenchman Aymar Du Rivail, who had studied at Pavia under the same masters as Alciatus, published his *Historia iuris civilis et pontificii*. He concentrated on the main account of 'the origin of law' in the Digest, the long fragment D.1.2.2, from Pomponius, and supplemented it by reference to Livy's account of the early republic. Du Rivail sought to reconstruct the contents of the Twelve Tables, and, since that legislation was said to be inspired by the Athenian laws of Solon, he included all the known provisions of Solon's law.

When they distinguished between the various strata of law represented in the Digest, the humanists recognised that the state of Roman law was related to the state of Roman society, and that as that society changed, so did the law. In particular they noted that the law of a particular period was affected by the political situation of the time. In charting the development of Roman law, they drew parallels with the political changes that were going on in contemporary France. Some thought that the study of ancient law might offer answers to their own constitutional problems. But the more they related Roman law to what they discovered about Roman society, the more they realised how different their sixteenth-century society was from the society of ancient Rome. That realisation led them in turn to question whether it was appropriate to seek to use Roman law as a model for contemporary France at all.

By stressing the connection between Roman law and ancient Roman society, the humanists were in effect challenging the claims of the Roman civil law to universal validity. The main exponent of this line of argument was François Hotman. He stressed the distinction between public law and private law, arguing that the public law of any country was necessarily related to its form of government. But even in private law, Roman law changed as society changed and many rules became obsolete. In his *Francogallia* (1573), he held that the France of this time was the product of Frankish, not Roman, institutions and that the Franks were a Germanic people untouched by Roman law. Hotman argued that French landholding was essentially governed by feudal law and that, despite the medieval incorporation of the *Libri feudorum* in the Corpus iuris, feudal law was quite alien to true Roman law. As he put it in his *Antitribonianus*, written in 1552 but published posthumously in 1603, a French lawyer entering a French court, equipped only with a knowledge of Roman rules of property and succession, would be as well qualified as if he had arrived among the American savages. Roman civil law was just inappropriate to sixteenth-century France.

Both the humanists' criticism of the texts of Roman law and their stress on the relationship of Roman law with ancient Roman society undermined the veneration in which the Corpus iuris had been held. Most of the humanists recognised that, for rational and equitable solutions to many perennial legal problems, the work of the classical Roman jurists was unrivalled. They felt free, however, for the first time to criticise the form in which those rulings were transmitted. The difficulties of discovering what was ancient Roman law were compounded by the obscure form in which the texts of the Corpus iuris were arranged. Neither the Digest nor the Code had a rational order and they contained many repetitions and antinomies. The result was that there was far too much scope for contradictory interpretations and, in the minds of ordinary citizens, civil lawyers had acquired a reputation for complex arguments, which served as an invitation to chicanery.

4 THE CIVIL LAW BECOMES A SCIENCE

The humanist professors at Bourges believed that law should be capable of being presented in the same way as other scientific disciplines, in particular by proceeding logically from what is universal to what is particular. Earlier jurists had been notoriously suspicious of this method and clung tenaciously to the traditional order of the texts. Cicero had become an idol of the humanists and already in antiquity he had pleaded, unsuccessfully, for a recasting of the civil law as a science (*ius civile in artem redactum*). The humanists were determined to fulfil Cicero's dream.

The only part of the Corpus iuris that was arranged in a rational order was the Institutes. It had not received great attention from the Commentators but henceforth it was to figure prominently in attempts to recast the civil law in more systematic form. The manifesto of the Bourges group was a short tract by François Duaren (Duarenus) on teaching and learning law (*Epistula de ratione docendi discendique iuris*, 1544). After castigating the customary teaching methods, he argued that law should be expounded in the same way as other sciences, by proceeding from what is universal and familiar to us to what is particular. To this end he commended the briefer and more systematic approach of the Institutes as superior to any other. Among the few humanists to move from the stage of planning programmes to that of producing actual re-arrangements were François Connan (Connanus), who died in 1551, and Hugues Doneau (Donellus) (1527–1591).

Connanus started from the Institutional division of the law into persons, things and actions, but he disposed of the material under those heads in a new way. The traditional order was rational insofar as it treated of the different capacities of persons and different kinds of things, but it ceased to be rational when it treated of actions. Connanus notes that under this head Justinian did not deal with legal procedure but included obligations as being introductory of actions. He deduces that 'actions' must include any act of a person which might lead to legal proceedings. So for him the category includes not only obligations but also marriages, which had traditionally been dealt with under the head of persons, and wills and intestate succession, which had previously been categorised under things. They all result from acts which had legal effects.

Donellus was less radical and more influential than Connanus. He assumed that Justinian's law must be logical, even though it did not appear to be so, and applied himself to identifying what he conceived to be its underlying rational structure. In view of the great influence of his work on the future development of the civil law, it is worth considering his argument in some detail.

Justinian's definition of law gives one aim for all law, namely to assign to each what is due to him (*suum cuique tribuere*). So divine law is concerned with what is God's, public law with what is the public's and private law with what belongs to private individuals. When the Roman jurists referred to civil law, however, they meant essentially private law, the subject of nearly forty-nine of the fifty books of the Digest and nearly nine of the twelve books of the Code. So Donellus saw his task as the analysis of a law that assigned to private individuals what was their *ius* in various situations. In Latin and most European languages the same word, *ius*, *Recht*, *droit*, is used to indicate both the objective law, for example, the law of obligations, and a subjective right, for example, the right to sell a thing, and this double meaning masks a potential ambiguity, which does not exist in English. For Donellus the word *ius* normally meant a subjective right appertaining to an individual, so that for him the law as a whole was a system of rights.

In analysing the institutional scheme, Donellus concentrated on the meaning of actions. He rejected Connanus's interpretation and observed that in general the Roman jurists used the word *actio* to mean a legal proceeding. He therefore criticised Justinian for joining actions with obligations. Donellus's conclusion was that the civil law consists, first, of knowing what in law belongs to each individual, and secondly, of the procedural means of obtaining it.

Previously the rules of law were not clearly distinguished from the particular remedies by which they were enforced. Now, for the first time, private law was divided into substantive law, on the one hand, conceived as a system of subjective rights, and civil procedure on the other. Logically the identification of what is legally due to each person must necessarily precede any discussion of the means for obtaining it. If that be so, then it must be wrong to begin the treatment of private law with a discussion of actions and judgments. Yet that is what the compilers of the Digest have done. The institutional system, by putting actions last, is therefore preferable.

The division between substantive law and procedure was the basis for Donellus's great Commentaries in twenty-eight books, of which the first sixteen were devoted to substantive law and the last twelve to civil procedure. The rights which comprise the substance of private law are divided into two categories, what is truly and properly ours and what is owed to us. The first category includes both the rights which we enjoy as free men, such as life and liberty, and also our rights over external things. The second includes rights derived from what another person is bound to do for us. Thus although obligations are not truly ours, in the sense that our reputation or our house is ours, yet they are still rights belonging to us.

Donellus sought to reproduce the substance of Justinian's law purged both of its original defects of form and of its medieval corruptions. For example, the Roman notion of ownership (*dominium*) was indivisible. The medieval treatment of the feudal relationship of lord and vassal, according to which ownership of the land was divided between lord and vassal, could not therefore be sustained. How then could the vassal's interest be recognised? Traditionally it had been seen as a special kind of usufruct, but since usufruct was limited to the life of the holder, that was inappropriate. Donellus noticed that, apart from usufruct, Roman law recognised a number of limited property interests in things owned by another, such as rights of way, rights of security, *emphyteusis* (a lease for a very long period, which accorded the lessee a property interest). He concluded that they were all reductions of the owner's rights and constituted a general category of property rights held by one person in another's property (*iura in re aliena*). Donellus was the first to recognise this notion, which was to become a cornerstone of the modern civil law of property and which might have covered the vassal's interest.

In their search for an ever more logical arrangement of the law, late-sixteenth-century jurists exploited the potentialities of printing through the use of extensive tabulation, advocated by the French logician Peter Ramus. The tables indicated in diagrammatic form the relationship between general and particular categories.

An influential example of the application of Ramist methods to law is the *Dicaeologicae lib. III* of the German scholar Johannes Althusius, which appeared in 1617. The sub-title indicates its aim: 'The whole law in force, methodically set out, with parallels from Jewish law, and supplemented by tables.' Althusius first distinguishes between law and facts, by which he means the transactions between persons which have effects in the law. Building on Connanus's idea that in the institutional scheme actions should be understood as covering not just legal proceedings but all human acts, Althusius developed the notion of the *negotium*. This category includes every transaction which affects the social life of man, either by adding something useful or necessary or by providing an obstacle to it. The *negotium* is classified into parts and species. The parts are, first, the objects with which the transaction is concerned, which are subdivided into corporeal and incorporeal and so on, and secondly, the persons involved in the transaction, who may be singular or collective, etc. The species are the types of transaction which may be voluntary acts, such as contracts, or involuntary acts, such as delicts. Substantially Althusius's discussion was based on the Roman civil law, but he subordinated the content to a form that owed little to Roman law.

5 THE ORDERING OF THE CUSTOMARY LAW

Humanist jurisprudence was not confined to the civil law. In the later fifteenth century much of the law applied by courts throughout Europe was essentially conceived as traditional custom. It was hardly affected at all by legislation but to a varying degree it was affected by the memory of the Roman law of antiquity and by the infiltration of the 'learned' law taught in the universities. The customs of the Italian states, and of Spain and of southern France, the *pays de droit écrit*, still carried some vestiges of the barbarised Roman law of the Visigoths and of the tradition of Roman law teaching along the Mediterranean littoral. In northern France, the *pays de droit coutumier*, the local customs were of Germanic origin, mainly Frankish, but the introduction of the Romano-canonical procedure had produced a class of professional lawyers, who applied to the customary law the methods of Roman and canon law. In Germany, however, the customary law was almost untouched by Roman law.

A few French customs had been put into written form, but in the absence of such a record, recourse had to be made to the folk-memory of the community and unless the scope of a particular custom was *notoire*, or recognised by all, an *enquête par turbe* was required, in which senior members of the community were interrogated about the custom in question. This was a costly and time-consuming procedure and from the middle of the fifteenth century the French kings sought to require local communities to record their law in writing. At first the royal commands were met by local inertia but then a procedure was devised which combined royal authority, the participation of professional lawyers and popular acceptance. Meetings of the local assemblies were convened to approve the formulation of the local custom. The government sent senior lawyers, usually judges of the provincial courts, the Parlements, to preside as royal commissioners. If any rule appeared to be unfair, it was criticised and could be reformed. The assemblies usually included professional lawyers, apart from the presiding commissioners, and as the discussions became more technical the professionals tended to take over the proceedings and to dictate the final outcome, although the assembly as a whole had to give its approval.

In the first half of the sixteenth century all the French regional customs were 'codified' in this way and, being now cast in authoritative and intelligible form, became the subject of academic comment and interpretation in the civil law manner. It became easier to identify what were the elements common to all or most of the customs. The most important exponent of the customs was Charles Dumoulin (Molinaeus) (1500–66). He studied at Orleans, where he was steeped in the traditional learning of Bartolus and Baldus. He also imbibed, however, much of the spirit of humanism and thus applied the Bartolist learning with a freer spirit than earlier writers. This was partly because, as a Protestant and nationalist, he had a vision of restoring the good old customary law that he considered to be a feature of an earlier, purer, France. In particular he rejected the Bartolist idea that written customs, *statuta*, which conflicted with the *ius commune*, should be given as narrow a construction as possible.

Dumoulin's main work was his Commentary on the Custom of Paris, which appeared in 1538. The custom had been given definitive form in 1510 and the commentary was written in Latin. Dumoulin's approach may be illustrated by his treatment of feudal tenures. He questioned the legal force of the *Libri feudorum* in the Corpus iuris. Their compiler Obertus had no official position and it was wrong to regard his collection as having the validity of Justinian's texts, although it had been so regarded for over three hundred years (*Opera omnia*, 1681, 1.115,815). When, however, he came to expound the detail of fiefs, as contained in the Custom of Paris, Dumoulin was prepared to use the traditional learning of the commentators. The main problems were the nature of the vassal's interest in the land and the nature of the vassal's duty to his lord.

Traditionally the categorisation of the vassal's interest was based on the description of Obertus, who stated that the vassal had the right to use and enjoy the land. To a civil lawyer, this made the vassal's interest sound like a civil law usufruct, but one which, unlike an ordinary usufruct, passed from generation to generation. Civil lawyers had also called the vassal's interest *dominium utile*, by contrast with the *dominium directum* of the lord. Dumoulin was content to accept this traditional understanding of the vassal's interest as giving the vassal a permanent usufruct.

So far as the vassal's duties to the lord were concerned, there had been a tendency to characterise them as merely variations of the debtor–creditor relationship. To treat feudal relationships as purely economic, however, was, in Dumoulin's view, to omit a significant aspect, namely the honour and respect due from the vassal to his lord, in addition to any payment that he might have been obliged to make. Dumoulin wanted to restore the true character of the feudal relationship and was able to exploit what at first sight might have seemed a trivial point, derived from the Commentators. Baldus distinguished between ordinary debts and debts due by vassal to lord, on the ground that in an ordinary debt the creditor had either to fix the place of payment contractually or else to come to the debtor to collect it, whereas the feudal debtor, since he owed respect to his lord, had to come to the creditor. Although the Custom of Paris was silent on the place of payment of feudal dues, Dumoulin insisted that feudal tenure required the vassal, as part of his duty of respect for his lord, to seek him out to make his payment. In this way Dumoulin used the learning of the civil law Commentators in an eclectic manner to combat the idea that the feudal relationship had become purely economic and to re-establish older notions, which in his view were part of the fabric of traditional French society.

In his *Oratio de concordia et unione consuetudinum Franciae* (*Omnia opera*, 1681, II.690), Dumoulin argued for the existence of an agreed core of rules, common to all customs, from which gaps in individual customs could be filled rather than from the civil law. This idea was taken up by Guy Coquille (1523–1602) in his *Institution au droit français*. Despite its comprehensive title, this work was concerned only with the fields of law dealt with in the customs and royal legislation and Coquille had to admit that, in order to fill gaps, it was sometimes necessary to have recourse to the civil law. The latter was, however, clearly a subsidiary law of last resort.

6 THE BARTOLIST REACTION

The ferment of humanist activity centred on Bourges affected civil law scholarship throughout the academic world and in the long term it transformed the civil law. Its immediate impact on the practice of the law, by contrast, was negligible. Court advocates and notaries everywhere remained faithful to the Bartolist tradition. This was not because they were unaware of the challenge of legal humanism. Civil lawyers had become a formidable political and social force in all societies. In France they were accepted as constituting a *noblesse de la robe* and resented any movement which appeared to subvert the expertise which furnished their qualification for positions of power in state and local government.

Apart from the challenge to their vested interests, however, the civil law practitioners found much of the humanist scholarship irrelevant to their daily concerns. The arguments that would carry weight with a court were not to be found in humanist discussions of what Ulpian actually meant but in the writings of Bartolus and Baldus and their successors. The commentaries, which so offended the aesthetic sensibilities of the humanists, followed a set pattern which practitioners readily mastered. Previous discussions were always carefully cited and fine distinctions drawn between different fact-situations. *Repertoria* abounded which enabled the practitioner to find what he was looking for and often he could skip the preliminaries and go straight to the discussion of the contemporary application of the law.

That the *mos italicus* flourished is evidenced by the spate of reprints of the Commentators' works, which throughout the sixteenth century poured from presses of printing houses not merely in Italy but also in Paris and Lyons. Indeed humanist works had only a small circulation, confined to scholars, and in modern libraries are rare compared with works on the *ius commune*. The latter now acquired its own apologists. By way of defence against reliance on the original meaning of a text, they developed the notion of the *communis opinio doctorum*. Baldus had argued that, if the main commentators were agreed on a particular doctrine, that opinion had the force of custom. Now it was said that it had greater authority than any particular text of the Corpus iuris itself. This was the ultimate triumph of the commentary over the text in a struggle which had begun with the glossators.

Alberico Gentili was an Italian Protestant, who studied law, entirely in the Bartolist tradition, at Perugia. Being forced to leave Italy for religious reasons, he arrived in England in 1580 and two years later published his *De iuris interpretibus dialogi sex*, a fierce defence of the Bartolist methods against the French humanist school. His argument was based on practical considerations. The purpose of teaching civil law is to prepare students for practice in modern society. Where, he asked, did the humanist professors expect their students to go after their studies, to Plato's Republic or to Utopia? (*Dialogus*, IV.)

7 THE RECEPTION OF ROMAN LAW

As the national states in continental Europe gloried in their new found 'sovereignty', and set up professional courts to take over important business from local courts, they uniformly adopted a variant of the Romano-canonical procedure. They adopted the substantive civil law, however, only to the extent that the existing customary law was inadequate for their needs or was difficult of access, since it had not been cast in written form. Thus in France, where the customary laws had generally been codified, the reception of Roman law into court practice proceeded as a gradual trickle, whereas in Germany, as we shall see, it was a dramatic flood. Sometimes royal legislation furthered the movement. In Spain the

Siete partidas acted increasingly as a counterweight to provincial particularism. In 1567 they were supplemented by a collection of new laws, known as the *Nueva Recopilación*, arranged in nine books in imitation of Justinian's Code.

Everywhere there was a need for the more comprehensive and technically superior law that was offered in Justinian's texts, but the extent of its adoption depended on the local circumstances. The situation in Britain illustrates the process of the reception. At the beginning of the sixteenth century, the northern part of the island, Scotland, had a customary law similar to that of England but far less developed, since, unlike England, it lacked both a central court of professional judges and a core of trained lawyers. In 1532 a permanent court of professional judges, the Court of Session, was set up and it adopted the standard continental written procedure. As far as possible, it applied traditional Scots law but in cases where no guidance was to be found in that law, the lawyers turned to the *ius commune*. An act of the Scots Parliament of 1583 refers to a civil law rule as 'the disposition of the common law', by which it meant not the English common law but the *ius commune*. Three universities, at St Andrews, Glasgow and Aberdeen, had been set up in the fifteenth century and they introduced the teaching of canon and civil law. It was usual, however, for budding Scots lawyers to study civil law on the continent, at first in France and from the late sixteenth century in the Netherlands. The Scottish courts always stressed that they adopted a civil law rule not because the civil law had any special authority in Scotland, but because of its 'equity', or rationality. As a source of law suited to the problems of sixteenth-century life, particularly those arising from the growth of commerce, there was no viable alternative.

The situation in England was more complex. After its flirtation with the civil law in the time of Bracton, the English common law had become a highly sophisticated discipline with a well-trained core of lawyers, who had studied at the Inns of Court in London, a legal university in all but name. It had, however, become inward-looking and resistant to change. One of its features was that, as in the formulary procedure of classical Roman law, almost the only remedy that the common law offered was money damages. When other remedies came to be needed, such as an injunction to a party to do something or not to do something, or rectification of a document, they had to be sought elsewhere. Litigants petitioned the chancellor, as 'the keeper of the king's conscience', to give them the relief that the common law courts could not provide. This jurisdiction of the Court of Chancery, administering rules which were collectively known as Equity, grew up in the fourteenth and fifteenth centuries.

Most of the pre-Reformation chancellors were ecclesiastics, familiar with canon and civil law, and they drew freely on them in developing Equity. For example, the principal institution of Equity is the trust, under which the legal owner of property is compelled to hold it for the benefit of another person, the 'equitable owner'. In working out the duties of trustees in regard to their management of trust property, the chancellors could find help in civil law discussions of the duties of tutors responsible for administering the property of wards under the age of puberty. Equity was therefore more open to civil law influence than the traditional common law.

England, of course, had its Church courts, applying canon law and procedure, and also certain courts which used the Romano-canonical procedure and directly applied the *ius commune*. The most important was the Court of Admiralty, which dealt with maritime disputes and other matters with an international character. The lawyers who accompanied the army on campaign in the capacity of judge-advocate also used the civil law, as did the courts of the vice-chancellors of the two English universities of Oxford and Cambridge.

The common lawyers had no right of audience in the courts of canon and civil law. The practitioners in those courts belonged to a guild, equivalent to the Inns of Court, called Doctors' Commons. It was these doctors to whom the government turned to conduct international negotiations. For the most part they received their training at Oxford and Cambridge. On severing the links with Rome, King Henry VIII abolished the formal teaching of canon law, although in practice the courts of the Church of England continued to apply it in matrimonial and testamentary matters and even took account of contemporary post-Reformation continental doctrine. The teaching of civil law, on the other hand, was strengthened and Henry chose it, together with other Renaissance subjects, such as Greek, Hebrew and Protestant theology, as the subjects of the Regius Chairs that he established in Oxford and Cambridge, the nomination for which was to be, and still is, in the Crown.

8 THE RECEPTION IN GERMANY

The early adoption of the Romano-canonical procedure in France and the incorporation of Roman terms and categories in the codified customs meant that much Roman law had gradually seeped into French law. Germany, on the other hand, for long seemed immune to its influence. It was a loose confederation of principalities and free cities united under the Holy Roman Emperor. Neither the royal concern for codification nor the widespread professional expertise, which characterised the French situation, were present. The courts of customary law were those of the Schöffen, groups of respected local laymen, whose legal work was only a part of their daily activity, and who transmitted their knowledge of the customs by word of mouth. Their procedure was informal and oral, evidence was based on the ancient method of compurgation (oath-helping). In their judgments they normally stated the facts and gave their conclusions without explaining how they had reached them. Their authority as custodians of the community's legal tradition depended on the respect in which they were generally held.

It was not until the late fifteenth century that this system was seriously challenged. From the thirteenth century Germans had studied law at universities in Italy and France and from the fourteenth century universities had been established in German-speaking lands. Prague, founded in 1348, was quickly followed by Vienna (1365), Heidelberg (1385), Cologne (1388) and several others, but at first their students were almost exclusively churchmen and if they taught the civil law at all, it was as subsidiary to canon law. Some elementary 'vocabularies' and nutshells of Roman law circulated in fifteenth-century Germany, suggesting that some acquaintance with at least the language of Roman law was regarded as useful for minor bureaucrats. The judges of the ecclesiastical courts, using the Romano-canonical procedure, sometimes acting as arbitrators rather than strictly as judges, had more to do than elsewhere in Europe. For in certain types of case litigants preferred professional judges and written procedure to lay judges and oral procedure.

As long as the Schöffen courts adhered to the traditional oral procedure, the influence of Roman law on the law in practice was necessarily slight. In the last decades of the fifteenth century, certain Schöffen courts, such as that in the free city of Frankfurt am Main, allowed the use of a form of the Romano-canonical procedure, with written pleadings, drafted by trained advocates. This change occurred without legislation and the initiative for it came from the litigants and their legal advisers. They found that the traditional procedure was inadequate for them to bring the issues involved before the court and the only alternative available to them was the procedure used in the Church courts. The old procedure was not immediately abolished but was soon superseded.

The procedural changes did not necessarily require the substitution of Roman law for the traditional customary law. After all in France the written procedure had for long been used in the courts applying customary law, without significantly affecting its substance, since both the judges and the advocates were normally trained jurists. In Germany, however, where the customs were uncodified, the untrained Schöffen found it difficult to cope with the sophisticated legal arguments, supported by citations from Roman law, which the litigants' advocates began to include in the written arguments that they pressed on the court. They turned for help either to the legally trained officials in the administration of their area or to the professors in the law faculty of the local university and these jurists were happy to exploit their special expertise in the learned law. They insisted on strict proof of unwritten custom and could disallow it, if it seemed irrational. It is significant that in Saxony, where the customary law had exceptionally been put into written form, the influence of Roman law was less than elsewhere. On the whole this influence was strongest in the law of obligations, particularly the law of contract, which was only sparsely dealt with in the customary law.

The practice of asking for advice from the law faculty of the local university was institutionalised when *Aktenversendung* became usual. The whole written record of the case was sent to the faculty, with a request for its collective opinion, which the court then felt obliged to follow. Apart from their greater expertise in the law, the professors were regarded as dealing with the case on a completely impartial basis. In the turbulent times of the sixteenth and seventeenth centuries the judges of the local courts were glad to be relieved of some of the responsibility for unpopular decisions. The practice received official encouragement in the imperial criminal law, the Carolina, issued by the Emperor Charles V in 1532. Its last article, 219, required judges, who were not learned or experienced in the imperial law, to seek advice 'at the nearest university, city or other source of legal knowledge'. As a result, the preparation of such opinions became a major activity of German law faculties. It brought academic law in touch with the practice of law but this advantage was sometimes offset by a decline in the quality of the professors' teaching and in their more reflective studies.

The ease and speed with which Roman law was received in Germany in the early sixteenth century were surprising. The motives were mainly practical, but the intellectual climate was right. The Renaissance interest in the heritage of classical antiquity flourished in Germany, and the German humanists did not separate themselves from the practice of the law as much as did their French counterparts. Inevitably, however, the law which was received had to be in a practical form acceptable to a court and that meant that the Reception was of the *mos italicus* rather than of the *mos gallicus*.

A contributing factor was the continuing force of the Holy Roman empire. The emperors recognised that the imperial law of the Corpus iuris, which had become a *ius commune* for much of Europe, could, if generally adopted, constitute a unifying factor for their diverse territories. They favoured the idea of a *translatio imperii*, a transfer of empire from ancient Rome to Germany. This was supposed to have been formally marked when the twelfth-century Emperor Lothar was persuaded by Irnerius (whose name may have been a variant of Werner) to adopt the Roman laws as his own, so that the empire became the Holy Roman Empire 'of the German nation'. The Lotharian legend was exploded by Hermann Conring in his *De origine iuris Germanici* in 1643.

The existence of civil law texts that supported absolute imperial power and that were cited by the bureaucrats whom the princely governments recruited, clearly did not diminish the favour with which the German princes regarded Roman law. The civil law offered the means of establishing a bureaucratic state, by which princes could counter the independence of over-mighty feudal lords. All over Europe law was beginning to be seen less as a set of traditional customary rules and more as legislation, issued in the name of the prince and interpreted by the supreme court for his dominions.

The supreme court for the Holy Roman Empire was the Reichskammergericht, in which the competing interests of the emperor and the leading princes were supposed to be balanced. Its jurisdiction was mainly appellate. In 1495 it was reformed to ensure that the sixteen judges were representative of the various powerful interests; half of them had to be of at least knightly status and the other half trained jurists. After 1548 all its members had to be trained jurists. The court adopted the Romano-canonical procedure and had to decide 'according to the common law of the empire and also the proper, worthy and accepted statutes and customs'. Proof of unwritten local custom was always difficult in practice and until the court built up its own court custom from its decisions, there was a continuing pressure to adopt the Roman rule as being the *ius commune* or *gemeines Recht* of the whole empire.

The reception of Roman law in Germany was not achieved without opposition. The social unrest of the sixteenth century, which manifested itself in such uprisings as the Peasants' War of 1524–5, was accompanied by complaints against the bureaucratic lawyers, who were the most visible representatives of government. To some extent this was not an attack on the civil lawyers specifically but an expression of the view of lawyers in general as the bulwark of the establishment and the opponents of reform. When Shakespeare depicted Jack Cade's Rebellion in England in 1450, he made Cade's collaborator say 'The first thing we do, let's kill all the lawyers', (*Henry VI*, Part 2, IV.2). In Germany, however, the arriviste civil lawyers, with their new practices, incomprehensible to laymen, and the fat salaries which they enjoyed, were further identified with the disappearance of the old ways. The temporal coincidence of the procedural reforms with the beginnings of the Reformation meant that the civil law and the canon law, both emanating from Rome, could be characterised as alien importations standing in the way of God's law, as expressed in Holy Scripture.

Jurists in Germany, as in Italy and France, had social pretensions, insisting that Doctors of Law were *milites legum*, legal knights, equal in status to military knights. They were viewed as seeking to stir up antagonism between disputing parties rather than solve the disputes peacefully. They could find a counter-argument, however specious, to any proposition that was advanced and took full advantage of the increased opportunities for appeals which the professional courts provided. They were regarded as a boon to the rich, who could pay for their services and so prolong legal proceedings indefinitely, but as a bane to the poor, who could often afford to be represented only by half-trained but glib impostors, falsely claiming to be learned jurists. As a class jurists were seen as unscrupulous and bad Christians (*Juristen böse Christen*) and there were many popular stories of how St Peter waited in vain at the gate of heaven for a jurist to appear.

Despite all this sound and fury, however, it was too late to put the clock back. The jurists of the civil law were there to stay. After some earlier wavering, influential figures such as Philip Melanchthon extolled the virtues of Roman law as standing above petty factionalism and as the only impartial law of peace and order.

9 COURT PRACTICE AS A SOURCE OF LAW

As courts became exclusively professional, they became more conscious of the civil and customary elements in the law that they applied. It was realised that each court had its own practice, which constituted a forensic custom, *usus fori*, the evidence for which could be found only in the court's decisions. Litigants therefore needed to have access to such decisions, particularly if the judgments were 'motivated', in the sense that the court gave its reasons for the decision and indicated what authorities it followed. The most prestigious court in Europe to give such judgments was the Rota Romana, which was not only an appellate tribunal for the Roman Catholic Church in all countries but also dealt with secular matters arising in the Papal States. Reports of the judgments of the Rota had been published since the fourteenth century, when the court was at Avignon. The first reporter was an English auditor (or judge), called Thomas Fastolf, who was familiar with the English practice of recording court proceedings in 'year-books'.

Where the secular courts did not give reasoned judgments, individual judges took it on themselves to collect and publish selected court decisions, which could then be printed. Guy Pape, a judge of the Parlement de Dauphiné at Grenoble, made a collection of decisions of the court, which were published posthumously in 1490. The Dauphiné was mainly an area of the *droit écrit*, and Pape's reports cite texts of civil and canon law and the commentaries thereon. The earliest collection of an Italian secular court was Matthaeus de Afflictis's volume of the *Decisiones Sacri Regii Consilii* of Naples, published in 1499.

The decisions of the Reichskammergericht were not 'motivated' and in 1563 Joachim Mynsinger, a former judge of the court, published *Singularium observationum iudicii imperialis camerae centuriae quattuor*, in which, to the initial displeasure of his fellow judges on the court, he explained the reasons for the court's decisions in selected cases. His aim was to enhance the reputation of the court by showing that, although it did not state its reasons for reaching its decisions, it did in fact take into account the best writers of the *ius commune*.

The maxim of the civil law, enunciated by Justinian, was *non exemplis sed legibus iudicandum* (C.7.45.13); judges should interpret the law and not just follow precedent. The early reports cite mainly civil law authorities, sometimes suggesting that the judges were flaunting their familiarity with the learned law. By the end of the sixteenth century, however, the reports routinely cite earlier decisions of the court as precedents, with the implication that the court, although not bound to do so, would normally follow them. The forensic custom established by each court, and evidenced in the reports collected by judges and advocates of the court, demonstrated the precise mixture of customary and Roman elements.

The only body that could state authoritatively what was received from

Roman law and what was rejected in a particular area was the supreme court for that area. A significant work that utilised the reports for this purpose was Philibert Bugnyon's *Legum abrogatarum et inusitatarum in omnibus curiis terris iurisdictionibus et dominiis regni Franciae* (1563), which region by region indicated the civil law texts that had not been received.

There was now a distinction between the *ius commune* and the *usus fori* of a region. This raised the question of the burden of proof in doubtful cases. Was the *ius commune* law unless it was shown to have been rejected by the court or was it only law if it could be shown to have been received? The point was the subject of much debate in seventeenth-century German writing. The arguments were based on Bartolist commentaries and centred around whether such custom should be treated as fact and provable in the same way as fact. Johan Schilter, in his *Praxis iuris Romani in foro Germanico*, first published in 1675, argued for a middle way. 'The whole force and spirit of Roman law with us today resides in its suitability for adoption.' The Reception had produced a general presumption that the *ius commune* applied, if it was suitable and if there was no specific local statute or recognised custom to the contrary. In the absence of a contrary practice, advocates ought to cite appropriate civil law texts to assist the court.

10 CIVIL LAW AND NATURAL LAW

Apart from the use of the *ius commune* in court practice, the civil law continued to form part of a Christian literary amalgam including also canon law and theology. The sixteenth century saw the appearance of unprecedented problems, which had to be confronted against the background of this thought. One of the most pressing problems involved the status of the indigenous inhabitants of the Spanish dominions in the New World. Franciscus Vitoria, a Dominican who was professor of theology at Salamanca, dealt with it in his *Relectiones de Indis*, written in 1532.

Hitherto the legal community conceived by scholars was confined to Christian countries under the twin powers of emperor and Pope. Vitoria rejected the claim of Pope Alexander VI in 1493 to have the power to divide the newly discovered lands between Spain and Portugal. In his view the emperor could not validly claim sovereignty over the whole world and the temporal sovereignty of the Pope did not extend to barbarians. Vitoria argued that the *ius gentium* of the Roman texts, in which it meant the law shared by all peoples, should be understood also as *ius inter gentes*, that is, a set of rules governing the relations between one people and another. This law was based not on a sharing of religious belief but on the nature of mankind. For *ius gentium* is defined, in Institutes 1.21, as what natural reason has laid down among all peoples. In Vitoria's view, therefore, the relations between Spain and her newly acquired dominions had to be governed by this general law of nations.

Vitoria rejected the argument, also based on Roman law, that these lands were *res nullius*, belonging to no one, and so available to the first occupier. On the contrary, the local Indians had full ownership of their land under natural law, although they were pagan. For even heretics do not lose their rights of ownership. The natural law that applies between nations allows the Spanish to travel freely and engage in trade but does not allow them to deprive the Indians of their land against their will or to attack them, even if they are unwilling to become Christian and are therefore in a state of mortal sin.

Vitoria's championing of the rights of the indigenous peoples of the New World was primarily based on justice and morality but his key arguments owed much to ideas derived from Roman law. They were developed by his successor at Salamanca, the Dominican Domenico Soto, by Diego Covarruvias, bishop of Segovia, who was both civilist and canonist, and particularly by the Jesuit Francisco Suarez. The latter's treatise *De legibus*, published in 1612, is the most sophisticated statement of the Spanish neo-Scholastic school. He asserted that the obligatory force of natural law was based on reason rather than on God's will (II.6), but observed that in practice what reason prescribed might vary according to the circumstances (II.14.12). Suarez rejected the Bartolist view that the prince was the delegate of the people and only held power according to the people's will. In his view the people transferred power to the prince absolutely and irrevocably (III.4). Logically the prince must be *legibus solutus* and cannot be bound even by his own laws. These Spanish scholastics developed the union of Aristotelian methods and Roman law begun by Aquinas. This enabled them to produce general theories, for example in regard to contractual liability, which had great influence on later writers. Their views had, however, very little effect on the actual practice of the colonists in the New World.

Later writers continued to separate the more general propositions to be found in the Roman texts from statements which were clearly applicable only to the civil law in its narrow sense. The more general propositions were identified with the law of nature and of nations and indeed several had been expressly attributed in the original texts to 'natural reason'. Since a virtuous man should act according to the principles of nature, such statements were held to be generally applicable not only as rules of law but also as principles of personal morality.

In the context of the law of nature and of nations a new importance was given to the maxims collected in the last title of the Digest (50.17): for example, no one ought to be enriched to the detriment of another (206); no one can transfer to another a better right than he has himself (54); no one is guilty of dishonesty who is exercising his own right (55); he who suffers loss due to his own fault is not considered to have suffered loss (203); in an equal case, the possessor must be considered the stronger party (128). Many of these remarks had been made by classical jurists as part of their justification of a particular ruling and had been converted into general maxims by the simple expedient of removing them from their context. As such they expressed truths that did not need to be justified; as when in English a statement is introduced by 'it stands to reason that', they were regarded as self-evident. Such maxims were highly regarded by those who wanted to present the law as a rational discipline, for they could serve as the general principles from which the logical deduction of detailed rules could be made. They provided a ready-made quarry from which moral philosophers could draw propositions with centuries of authority to support them.

11 CIVIL LAW AND INTERNATIONAL LAW

The burgeoning nation-states of the sixteenth century required the development of a public international law (*ius inter gentes*), as proposed by Vitoria. But the divisive effect of the Reformation on what had seemed to be a community of Christian peoples meant that such a law had to be separated from theology. In all European countries diplomacy had traditionally been in the hands of the civil lawyers, who could negotiate with each other on the basis of a commonly held set of legal ideas. One of the first writers to deal with the law governing the relations between states was the Italian Bartolist who had settled in England, Alberico Gentili.

In 1584 the Spanish ambassador to the court of Queen Elizabeth, Don Bernadino de Mendoza, was shown to have been implicated in a plot to free Mary, Queen of Scots, from prison and make her Queen of England. The Privy Council wanted to punish Mendoza but consulted Gentili as to the legal position. He advised that the criminal immunity of ambassadors under the civil law prevented any such punishment and so Mendoza was merely deported. Soon afterwards Gentili published the first treatise specifically devoted to a topic of international law, *De legationibus*. In this work Gentili gives an account of ambassadorial practice from Roman times and particularly of the Roman law of international relations, the *ius fetiale*. He discusses texts from the Corpus iuris but carefully distinguishes between the civil law and the law of nature and of nations. International law, he urged, is founded on the latter. In 1587 Queen Elizabeth made Gentili Regius Professor of Civil Law at Oxford and in the next few years he wrote several essays on the law of war, which were published together in Hanau in 1598 under the title *De iure belli, lib. III*. Gentili thus began the process of creating international law as a distinct discipline out of civil law materials. The process was completed a generation later by Grotius.

12 THEORY AND PRACTICE IN THE NETHERLANDS

The Low Countries in the fifteenth century formed part of the dominions of the dukes of Burgundy and in the sixteenth century fell to Charles V, who was duke of Burgundy and king of Spain, as well as emperor. The second half of the sixteenth century was marked by a series of revolts against the Spanish governors and the eventual breakaway of the seven northern provinces, which in 1579 formed the Union of Utrecht. Each province retained its own courts and particular law, but Holland, which produced over half of the wealth of the United Provinces, was the leader. Amsterdam replaced Antwerp as the main trading centre, through which the trade of the Rhine valley passed, and its merchants eventually came to dominate the commerce of the world.

Even before formal independence, the first university of the northern provinces was set up in 1575 at Leyden in Holland, to offer a Protestant counterweight to Louvain in the Catholic southern Netherlands. There, as in Spain itself, the Inquisition had increasingly repressed the dissemination of any ideas which seemed to threaten the traditional order of things. From the beginning the faculty of law at Leyden was given an important place in the university. At the formal opening procession, the Holy Scripture and Four Evangelists were followed by four Roman jurists: Julian, Papinian, Ulpian and Tribonian.

The main provinces other than Holland, were not to be outdone and universities with law faculties were founded at Franeker in Friesland in 1585, Groningen in 1614, Utrecht in 1636 and Hardewijk in Gelderland in 1648. The law of the United Provinces was largely created by the Dutch professors, particularly those of Leyden, and by the judges of the

High Courts of the provinces, particularly the Hooge Raad of Holland. Through their synthesis of legal science and legal practice, the Netherlands led the rest of Europe in the seventeenth century in the way that France had set the pace in the sixteenth.

In its early years Leyden was able to attract the French Protestant humanist Hugo Donellus, after his flight from France. He taught there from 1579 to 1587 and was succeeded by Everard Bronchorst, who had received his training in German universities. He set the tone which was to characterise the law of the Dutch universities. This was a combination of what became known as the 'elegant' and the 'forensic' approaches to law, in effect a moderate amalgam of the *mos gallicus* with the *mos italicus*. Students were to be prepared for court practice but they should first be inducted into the principles of all law.

Bronchorst stressed the importance for the student of law, at the beginning of his studies, to learn the basic principles of law which were to be found in the last title of the Digest and in the Institutes. For him the *regulae* of Digest 50.17 were the first principles of law, equivalent to the maxims of the dialecticians, the *problemata* of geometricians and the aphorisms of medical men. 'They cover in a brief compendium all the matters which are discussed at length in the vast ocean of the law and provide a general index of universal law.' Court advocacy was taught through *disputationes*, in which students could refer to the commentators of the Bartolist tradition.

The greatest product of the Leyden law faculty was Hugo Grotius (1583–1645), a child prodigy who entered the faculty at the age of eleven. Although not taught directly by Donellus, he was certainly influenced by his teaching. He completed his studies at Orleans, where he took his doctorate. As a result of his involvement in a theological dispute with political implications, he was imprisoned and used his enforced leisure to write, in Dutch, an Introduction to the jurisprudence of Holland (*Inleidinge tot de Hollandsche rechtsgeleerdheit*), finally published in 1631. In this work Grotius treated the law of Holland as a system of its own. It was no longer just an appendix of the civil law but an amalgam of Germanic custom and Roman law and subject to legislation, which was not to be accorded the narrow interpretation of a local *statutum*. In the tradition of Donellus, Grotius dealt only with substantive law and not with procedure. In order to retain the tripartite division of the Institutes, he divided the law into persons, things and obligations. After escaping from captivity, Grotius had to spend the rest of his life as a political refugee, mainly in France, where he was ambassador of Sweden.

In 1625 he published in Paris his most famous work, *De iure belli ac pacis*. In this treatise, Grotius, following ideas adumbrated by Suarez and Gentili, based international law firmly on a natural law, derived from the nature of man, which claimed to be independent of the civil law. The basic principles of this law were axiomatic and self-evident. Grotius said that, in developing his ideas on law, he had abstracted his mind from every particular fact, in the same way that mathematicians consider their figures abstracted from bodies (*prolegomena*, 58). The rules of natural law could be worked out in two ways, *a priori*, by logical deduction from the basic principles, or *a posteriori*, by observation of rules which were in practice common to the laws of all civilised peoples. For if a rule was everywhere accepted as law, that was good evidence of its origin in the natural reason that was shared by all mankind. Grotius preferred the latter method and illustrated the precepts of natural law with a wealth of examples. What natural reason prescribed often turned out to be what was set out or what could be inferred from Justinian's texts.

Grotius's treatise bristles with references to civil law texts, adduced to support propositions which claimed to be natural law. Grotius stressed that this law was not dictated by God, for, as he put it, it would exist even if we were to accept that there is no God or that human affairs were of no concern to Him (*prolegomena.* 11 and 1.1.10.5.). Thus Roman notions of occupation of things belonging to no one were adapted to the conquest of new territories and Roman contract law to international treaties. Natural law was presented as an extension or fulfilment of Roman civil law. The latter did not regard all promises as binding but in natural law every serious promise was binding and so treaties, once concluded, must be upheld. The maxim was *pacta sunt servanda*.

Grotius's contemporary Arnold Vinnius studied at Leyden and remained there as professor. It was he who established Dutch legal science as a mixture of Roman, customary and natural law elements. Vinnius made his name with his comprehensive commentary on Justinian's Institutes, which claimed to be both academic and forensic. In this work, which appeared in 1642, he wove together the ideas of the leading French humanists, such as Cujacius and Hotman, with those of the glossators and Bartolists and the more recent exponents of German court practice, such as Mynsinger. Furthermore, although his work purported to be devoted to an exposition of Justinian's Institutes, it referred to Dutch legal practice, cited from the collection of decisions of the Grand Council of Malines (in the southern Netherlands). Vinnius also made use both of Grotius's *Inleidinge* and his *De iure belli ac pacis*. The encyclopedic nature of Vinnius's book, cast in the familiar institutional scheme, made it a work of reference until the end of the eighteenth century. Vinnius also published a shorter version, or *Notae*, intended exclusively for students, that aimed to explain the Institutes, according to the best humanist ideas, but with little reference to practice. A hundred years later the short Notes were recommended by Lord Mansfield in England as the best introduction to Roman law for a gentleman and were read by John Adams, later the second President of the United States, when a student at Harvard College.

Vinnius was an eclectic writer, who sought to present Roman civil law as a source of the basic notions of universal law derived from nature, on the one hand, and of legal practice, on the other hand. Other writers concentrated their attention more specifically on the law of the United Provinces and marked the extent to which it differed from the pure civil law. Simon Groenwegen van der Made went through the whole of the Corpus iuris and carefully noted which texts had been rejected or ignored in practice. Following the model of the Frenchman Bugnyon a century earlier, he published his results in a treatise on what was not the law (Leyden 1649). Three years later his contemporary Simon van Leeuwen published *Paratitula iuris novissimi, dat is Een kort begrip van het Rooms-Hollandts Reght*, thus coining the title Roman-Dutch law, by which the law of the United Provinces and their colonies became known.

So far as private law was concerned, the work of the seventeenth-century Dutch school was synthesised in magisterial fashion by Johannes Voet, another Leyden professor, in his *Commentarius ad Pandectas*, published in two folio volumes in 1698 and 1704. Although he follows the order of the Digest titles, Voet arranged the material within each title quite differently. First the Roman law is explained and then the modern law, with full citation of the relevant authorities. Natural law, largely taken from Grotius, is mentioned but has only a modest place.

Perhaps the most innovative of the Roman-Dutch jurists was Ulrich Huber, who belonged not to Holland but to Friesland, where Roman civil law was received more than in other provinces. In his *De iure civitatis lib. III*, published in 1672, he built up, largely from Roman materials, a law of the state, which he called the 'new discipline of a universal public law'. In his *Praelectiones iuris civilis*, published between 1678 and 1690, he created, again out of Roman materials, the modern discipline of conflicts of laws, for dealing with cases involving different private laws. In his *Heedendaegse Rechtsgeleertheyd*, of 1698, building on Grotius's

Inleidinge, but with reference to Frisian practice, he gave an account of current law and with a wealth of detail set the law firmly in its social setting.

The widespread respect shown throughout Europe for the Dutch masters is attested by the large numbers of foreign editions of their main works in the later seventeenth and eighteenth centuries. Thus Bronchorst's commentary on Rules of Law had fourteen editions in Germany, France and the southern Netherlands. Vinnius's Commentary on the Institutes had nine editions in Lyons alone between 1666 and 1777, together with twelve in Venice between 1712 and 1804, three in Naples, five in Valencia and a translation into Spanish (Barcelona, 1846–7). Voet's Commentaries on the Digest received seventeen editions in France, Germany, Italy and Geneva and a translation into Italian in six volumes (Venice, 1837–40).

By the end of the seventeenth century Roman civil law had permeated the Protestant culture of northern Europe as much as it had previously formed part of Catholic Europe. This is shown by the proliferation of short summaries designed to popularise the essential aspects of the subject, especially the Institutes, and to help students to memorise them; some were expressed in aphorisms and even in verse. The immensity of the Digest demanded a different approach and efforts were made to harness the power of pictorial images to spread a knowledge of the range of matters covered in it. Johannes Buno's *Memoriale iuris civilis romani*, published in Hamburg in 1673, is the most ambitious and illustrates with detailed engravings the subjects of all the books of the Digest. The following year Buno supplemented it with a similar volume for the Code, Novels and *Libri feudorum*. In Friesland, where there was a tradition of pictorial tile making, Sybrant Feytema produced in the 1680s a series of tiles illustrating various Digest titles, each tile prominently marked with the number of the relevant title. As with Bruno's engravings, the tiles make no effort to portray the legal material in its original Roman setting but place it squarely in the familiar world of the late seventeenth century, the clothes of the participants, their weapons and their houses being obviously from northern Europe.

FURTHER READING

Works cited at the end of chapter 3; A. Watson, *The Making of the Civil Law*, Cambridge, Mass. 1981; H. Coing, *Europäisches Privatrecht, 1500–1800*, Munich 1985.

4.1. Bartolo da Sassoferrato, *Studi e documenti per il VI Centenario*, Milan 1962; P. Stein, 'Bartolus, the Conflict of Laws and the Roman law', in *Multum non Multa: Festschrift K. Lipstein*, ed. P. Feuerstein and C. Parry, Heidelberg 1980 (=*Character* 83); G. Vismara, 'La revoca del testamento giurato nella dottrina da Guglielmo Durante a Bartolo da Sassoferrato', in *Etudes du droit canonique dediées à G. Le Bras*, Paris 1965, II.1007.

4.2. D. Maffei, *Gli inizi dell'umanesimo giuridico*, Milan 1956.

4.3. P. Stein, 'Legal humanism and legal science', *TvR*, 54 (1986), 297 (=*Character*, 91); D. Osler, 'Budaeus and Roman law', *Ius Commune* 13 (1985), 195; S. Rowan, *Ulrich Zasius. A Jurist in the German Renaissance*, Ius Commune Sonderhefte 31, Frankfurt 1987; J.-L. Ferrary, 'Aymar Du Rivail et ses "Historiae iuris civilis et pontificii libri quinque"', *Bulletin de la Société Nationale des Antiquaires de France* (1992), 116; D. R. Kelley, *Foundations of Modern Historical Scholarship: Language, Law and History in the French Renaissance*, New York 1970; D. R. Kelley, *François Hotman*, Princeton, N.J. 1972.

4.4. J. P. Dawson, 'The codification of the French customs', *Michigan Law Review*, 38 (1940), 780; J. Q. Whitman, 'The Seigneurs descend to the rank of creditors', *Yale Journal of Law and the Humanities*, 6 (1994), 249.

4.5. P. Stein, 'Donellus and the origins of the modern civil law', in *Mélanges F. Wubbe*, Fribourg 1993, 439; D. van der Merwe, 'Ramus, mental habits and legal science', in *Essays on the History of Law*, ed. D. P. Visser, Cape Town 1989, 32.

4.6. D. Panizza, *Alberico Gentili, giurista ideologo nell' Inghilterra elisabettiana*, Padua 1981.

4.7. P. Stein, 'The influence of Roman law on the law of Scotland', *Juridical Review* (1963), 205 (=*Character*, 319); *The Civilian Tradition and Scots Law*, ed. D. L. Carey Millar and R. Zimmermann, Berlin 1997; R. Zimmermann, 'Der europäische Character des englischen Rechts', *Zeitschrift fur Europäisches Privatrecht*, 1 (1993), 4; R. H. Helmholz, *Roman Canon Law in Reformation England*, Cambridge 1990.

4.8. J. P. Dawson, *The Oracles of the Law*, ch. 3, Ann Arbor, Mich. 1968; W. Kunkel, 'The Reception of Roman law in Germany: an interpretation', in *Pre-Reformation Germany*, ed. G. Strauss, London 1972; G. Strauss, *Law, Resistance and the State: The Opposition to Roman Law in Reformation Germany*, Princeton 1986.

4.9. *Judicial Records, Law Reports and the Growth of Case Law*, ed. J. H. Baker, Berlin 1989; P. Stein, 'Civil Law Reports and the case of San Marino', in *Römisches Recht in der europäischen Tradition: Symposion F. Wieacker*, ed. O. Behrends, M. Diesselhorst and W. E. Voss, Ebelsbach 1985, 323 (=*Character*, 115).

4.10. *La seconda Scolastica nella formazione del diritto privato moderno*, ed. P. Grossi (Per la storia del pensiero giuridico moderno), Florence 1973; A. P. D'Entrèves, *Natural Law: An Introduction to Legal Philosophy*, 2nd edn, London 1970.

4.11. K.-H. Ziegler, *Völkerrechtsgeschichte*, Munich 1994.

4.12. *Das römische-hollandische Recht: Fortschritte des Civilrechts im 17. und 18. Jahrhundert*, ed. R. Feenstra and R. Zimmermann, Berlin 1992; R. Feenstra and C. J. D. Waal, *Seventeenth-century Leiden Law Professors*, Amsterdam 1975; G. C. J. J. Van den Bergh, *The Life and Work of Gerard Noodt (1647–1725): Dutch Legal Scholarship between Humanism and Enlightenment*, Oxford, 1988; J. E. Spruit, *Le droit romain, sujet d'une decoration murale du 17e siècle*, Arnhem 1989.

CHAPTER 5

Roman law and codification

I ROMAN LAW AND NATIONAL LAWS

In 1653 there appeared a book by the English civilian Arthur Duck on the use and authority of the Roman civil law in the realms of Christian princes (*De usu et authoritate iuris civilis Romanorum in dominiis principum Christianorum*). It is based on precise information about the extent to which the civil law had been received in different European countries and Duck was at pains to bring out the common ideas on the nature of law that those countries shared. Wherever one does not look merely at custom but seeks equity, he says, the laws of no nation are more suited than the civil law of the Romans, which contains the fullest rules concerning contracts, wills, delicts, judgments and all human actions.

The exact extent of the civil law component varied from country to country. Court practice (*usus fori*), as evidenced by collections of decisions, had for long reflected the particular amalgam of Roman civil law and customary law of the country or region. University teaching, on the other hand, had always remained tied to the civil law and ignored the customary element. By the middle of the seventeenth century the universities had to come to terms with the civil law as it was understood locally, and law faculties recognised national compounds of Roman and local law. In 1650 Michael Wexionius, professor in the university of Åbo (Turku) in Finland, then part of the Swedish kingdom, published an introduction to the study of Roman-Swedish civil law (*iuris civilis Sveco-Romani*). It was, however, as we have seen, the Dutch professors who most intensively developed a national law. In van Leeuwen's book of 1664, that was called Roman-Dutch law, since it was based partly on Roman and partly on Dutch sources.

In German countries, as in the Netherlands, seventeenth-century scholars also began to identify a particular German version of Roman law. Georg Adam Struve published an attempted synthesis in his

Jurisprudentia Romano-Germanica forensis in 1670 and about the same time the Austrian Nicholaus von Beckmann published a *Jus novissimum Romano-Germanicum* (1676). In the eighteenth century, however, German writers generally abandoned synthesis and emphasised the distinct character of the Roman elements, the German customary elements, and, especially in the Austrian provinces, the statutory elements in the national laws. Once the Roman and native elements were separated, the search began for a *ius germanicum commune*, based entirely on German sources, and as a result the Roman law elements took on a more alien appearance. Except for the use of the institutional scheme as a common form of presentation, the works on German law made no reference to Roman law, even as a subsidiary law for the filling of gaps.

One of the most widely read German jurists was Johann Gottlieb Heineccius (1681–1741). He was a Romanist, who was influenced by the later Roman-Dutch writers, but rejected their synthetic treatment in favour of a purely antiquarian approach to Roman law. His *Antiquitatum Romanarum syntagma*, first published in 1719, went through twenty editions. It illustrated, with much curious detail from ancient sources, the working of the various institutions of Roman law, according to the order of Justinian's Institutes, but it did not seek to show how those institutions had developed after Justinian or how they related to contemporary law. This was not because Heineccius had no interest in contemporary law, since he also published separate elementary accounts of modern civil law, German law and natural law. Each had become a distinct system of law.

In France, partly because of the distinction between the regions of the customary law and those of the written law, customary law had traditionally been kept separate from Roman law. The movement to provide a written record of the various distinct customs had fossilised them and efforts were made to identify a common core of customary law, based on the custom of Paris, which was distinct from the romanised customs of the south. In 1679 Louis XIV established in the universities royal professors of French law, who had to teach in the vernacular rather than in Latin. They tended to expound a generalised law based on the customs which were strongest in their region, but included also those parts of Roman law which had been received by the relevant regional Parlements. Such a Roman component was particularly marked in the law of obligations.

Between 1667 and 1681, Jean Baptiste Colbert, chancellor of Louis XIV, ordered the compilation of a series of mini-codes, in the form of

Royal Ordinances, which applied to the whole kingdom and so served to offset the centrifugal effect of the different customs. They were concerned with the least Roman parts of the law: with civil procedure, which Donellus had shown to be distinct from substantive law, with criminal law and criminal procedure, and with mercantile law.

Criminal law was dealt with to a limited extent in Books 47 and 48 of the Digest, which Justinian called *libri terribiles*, but the seventeenth-century version was badly in need of reform. Mercantile law figured significantly in the Roman texts, but had not been much developed in the middle ages. Merchants preferred to have their disputes settled not by local courts but by informal panels of their fellow merchants, which were set up at the periodical fairs, held in various towns, and in seaport towns where merchants congregated. So the mercantile community had developed a body of commercial custom which transcended national frontiers. Colbert engaged a successful businessman, Jacques Savary, to draft the *Ordonnance de commerce* (1673), an almost complete statement of rules for the conduct of business between merchants, based on these traditional customs. It was supplemented by a companion ordinance dealing with maritime commerce (1681). Thereafter French merchants, in whatever region they lived, followed a uniform law, which came to be accepted as an authoritative statement of commercial practice not only in France but also elsewhere in Europe, including England.

The Royal Ordinances did not significantly affect the core civil law, the subjects treated in Justinian's Institutes, and left the customs largely intact, but it defined their limits. Their effect was formally to hive off procedure, criminal law and mercantile law from the civil law and to that extent to circumscribe the scope of what was understood as the civil law.

In Spain the individual territories still retained their own laws and until the eighteenth century a national law was only a dream. Just as in France the custom of Paris gained ascendancy over other regional customs, so the law of Castille, based on the *Siete partidas* and the *Recopilación* of 1567, gradually became a national law (*derecho patrio*) for the whole of Spain. In 1713 the Council of Castille ordered that the universities should cease to teach Roman law and replace it with national law but the professors refused to implement the decree. In 1741 the Council issued a new decree allowing Roman law, in view of its great value, to be taught together with national law.

The standard textbook was Vinnius's Commentary on the Institutes, which was modified in two ways; first, references which were held to be offensive by the Inquisition, such as part of the treatment of marriage, were excluded, and secondly, references to Spanish law were inserted. Juan Sala produced for Spanish students an edition of *Vinnius castigatus* (Valencia, 1767), which claimed to achieve both aims. The frontispiece depicts Justice handing Justinian's Institutes to the emperor with her left hand and the *Siete partidas* to the King of Spain with her right hand.

2 THE MATURE NATURAL LAW

The later seventeenth century saw the further development of the civil law in the form of natural law. In the earlier part of the century the whole of Europe was wracked by warfare and there was a yearning for an impartial law that transcended human passions and antagonisms. Many writers felt that if only the content of Roman law could be released from the formal straitjacket in which it was imprisoned, Roman law might supply that need. G. W. Leibniz, who was a mathematician, jurist and philosopher, argued in his *Nova methodus discendae docendaeque jurisprudentiae*, published in 1667, that an order of treatment corresponding to nature must be geometrical. It must start from first truths, it must draw their direct consequences and, moving from consequence to consequence, arrive at a purely logical system. In his view the solutions of the Roman jurists were unsurpassed for their reasoning power but Justinian's compilation suffered from several defects. It contained too much that was superfluous, defective, obscure and confused. Indeed Leibniz devoted much effort to the production of a *Corpus iuris reconcinnatum*, in which the texts were re-arranged in a more logical order.

Sometimes statements taken from Justinian's texts were held out as general truths which applied even outside a legal context. Leibniz himself is fond of quoting such statements, in the context of moral discourse. For example, in his *Codex iuris gentium* of 1693 he says,

> The doctrine of law, taken from nature's strict confines, presents an immense field for human study. But the notions of law and justice, even after having been treated by so many illustrious authors, have not been made sufficiently clear. Right is a kind of moral possibility and obligation a moral necessity. By moral I mean that which is equivalent to natural for a good man: for, as a Roman jurisconsult has well said, we ought to believe that we are incapable of doing things which are contrary to good morals. (*Political Writings*, trans. P. Riley, Cambridge 1972, 170–1)

This is a strange observation, for clearly we do believe that we are capable of acting against morality. The jurist to whom Leibniz refers is Papinian and the text D.28.7.15. The original legal problem concerned a will in which the testator instituted his son as heir, subject to a condition. The rule was that such a condition was valid only if the son had the power to carry it out. An institution subject to a condition which he was unable to carry out was regarded as a failure to institute him, so that the whole will failed. Papinian's problem concerned the effect of a condition which required the son to do something immoral. Papinian held that such a condition invalidated the will as if it were a condition not within the son's power. He explained his ruling with the remark that 'it should not be understood that we have the power to do acts which harm our social duty and . . . are contrary to good morals'.

Papinian's concern was that the law should not both condemn an act and also require the doing of that act as a means of satisfying a condition. That is how his statement had been explained by Cujacius, for example, who calls it 'an expression worthy of a Christian' (*In lib. XVI quaestionum Pap. Comment., Opera Omnia* 1614, IV.346). In the intellectual climate of the seventeenth century, however, a jurist such as Papinian, although a pagan, was seen as an upholder of the unchanging moral character of law. As he had suffered for his beliefs, when he refused to condone the Emperor Caracalla's murder of his brother, the poet Andreas Gryphius in 1659 made Papinian the hero of a moralist drama.

The identification of natural law with moral philosophy was confirmed by Samuel Pufendorf, whose appointment to the first chair in the Law of Nature and of Nations (in the faculty of philosophy at Heidelberg in 1661) marked the formal recognition of natural law as a distinct discipline. Unlike Grotius, Pufendorf insisted on the specifically Christian character of natural law and switched its emphasis from natural rights to natural duties. Just as the humanist systematisers of the previous century had drawn inspiration from Cicero's proposal to convert the civil law into a science, so Pufendorf found a model in Cicero's treatise on duties (*De officiis*). His main work is a vast treatise on the law of nature and of nations, but his general influence was exerted more through his shorter and avowedly popular work *De officio hominis et civis iuxta legem naturalem* (On the duty of man and the citizen according to natural law), published in 1673. In this work he abandoned the familiar scheme of the Institutes and, although he retained the Roman categories, he presented them in a different order.

Dealing first with man's duties as a man, Pufendorf argued that, by making man a social and rational being, God created a natural law for him, which was expressed in the Gospel injunctions to love God and to love one's neighbour as oneself. Man as a man thus has three basic duties, to God, to himself and to other men. They form the first principles from which all detailed rules must logically follow. The first duty of man to other men is the obligation that arises when he gives his word to another. Subsequently come his duties in regard to the property of others and the contracts that concern property, especially sale. As a citizen, man's duties arise from the associations to which he belongs, ranging from the household to the state. The relationships that derive from the household are those of husband and wife, parent and child and master and servant (in a pre-industrial society, servants were considered more as family than as subjects of a contract of employment).

The search for a natural order deduced geometrically from Christian principles was vigorously continued by the French scholar Jean Domat in *Les lois civiles dans leur ordre naturel* (1689–94). For Domat, 'the order of society is preserved in all places by the engagements with which God links men together and that is perpetuated at all times by successions, which call certain persons to succeed, in the place of those who die, to everything that may pass to successors'. At the beginning he states certain principles that apply over the whole area of private law. These are taken from the opening title of the Digest (1.1.10): one should not harm another and one should render to each his due.

Persons and things are reduced to a brief description of different kinds of persons and things as they exist in nature and according to the civil law. The rest of private law is then grouped around the two heads of obligations (engagements) and successions. Obligations may be voluntary and involuntary. The first category includes not only contractual obligations but also those arising from usufructs and praedial servitudes. The second category includes delictal obligations. The natural lawyers reduced the various kinds of delict in Roman law to the general principle that one was liable for all loss caused to another by one's wilfulness or fault. Involuntary obligations also, however, included personal duties that Justinian's Institutes classed as quasi-contractual. They were essentially all personal duties not falling under the heads of contract, delict or quasi-delict, and included the duties of tutors to their wards and the duties of common owners to each other, which had previously been treated under the heads of persons and property respectively. Domat also subsumes under the head of obligations those legal elements which supplement obligations, such as real and personal security, possession and prescription. The other main part of private law, successions, more predictably deals with wills and intestacy and testamentary institutions, such as trusts (*fideicommissa*). Curiously, Domat's scheme was to have more following in Germany than in France and is the ancestor of the later Pandectist order and of the German civil code.

In the first half of the eighteenth century, natural law became even more abstract, a series of logical deductions from the rational and social nature of man. The most prominent exponents were the Germans Christian Thomasius (1655–1728) and Christian Wolff (1679–1754). Thomasius played down the utility of Roman law, arguing that barely a twentieth part of the Digest had any application in German courts and those parts which did have a practical relevance were essentially derived from natural law. Thomasius deplored the blurring of the distinction between law and morality and held that natural law constituted pieces of advice (*consilia*) to the enlightened ruler, who would supply the element of compulsion that turned them into law. Wolff, on the other hand, produced an elaborate mathematical system of natural law, as a series of moral duties, all rationally deduced from general moral principles, that were owed by everyone in society (*Ius naturae methodo scientifica pertractatum*, 8 parts 1740–8).

3 THE CODIFICATION MOVEMENT

In the eighteenth century the Roman civil law was caught up in the great intellectual movements of the Enlightenment. The rationalist natural law philosophy proclaimed that a complete set of laws could be stated simply and rationally, with existing complexities eliminated, and all that was needed to enact it was the will of the prince. The rulers were concerned to consolidate their power over their various domains, each with a different amalgam of Roman and customary law, and saw the imposition of a single code of law for all their territories as a means of unifying them. They also saw codification as a way of limiting the independence of the courts, whose judges often represented the entrenched interests of the provincial aristocracy. Codification was further urged on the princes by mercantilist thinkers who argued that commerce was impeded by the diversity of laws and would benefit from a uniform law.

The eighteenth-century concept of a code was not just the committal of the existing law to writing in a clear and systematic order. A code was usually intended to replace old rules that had become outmoded with a new modern law, suited to the needs of the time. In considering what to retain and what to reject of the old laws, however, the codification movement made people conscious of the origin of the various elements in the different laws that were being synthesised. At first the Roman civil law occupied a prominent position in the minds of the codifiers but, as the century went on, its continued relevance came to be questioned. Roman civil law came to be viewed less as a timeless *ius commune* or natural law and more as the law of an ancient society, set in a period that was very different from the age of Enlightenment.

The late eighteenth-century attitude to Roman law was affected by the success of Montesquieu's *De l'esprit des lois*, published in 1748. Montesquieu challenged the abstract rationalist form of natural law, from which Roman elements had largely been squeezed out, but his views did little to support greater reference to Roman law. He begins with the reassuring observation that laws in general are 'the necessary relations arising from the nature of things' and that human laws are the result of the application of reason. He then points out, however, that the nature of things, to which reason must be applied, differs from society to society. Laws cannot be universal but must be relative to the climate, economy, traditions, manners, religion, and so on, prevailing in a particular society. These factors together form 'the spirit of the laws' of that society, which the legislator ignores at his peril. Montesquieu used many examples from Roman law to illustrate his thesis but most of his readers must have drawn the conclusion that Roman law reflected the spirit of an ancient society, which was manifestly different from that of contemporary societies.

4 EARLY CODIFICATIONS IN GERMANY AND AUSTRIA

The first efforts to codify a state's law were made in the German-speaking countries. The earliest completed codes were those of the Duchy of Bavaria and were the work of one man, W. X. A. von Kreittmayr, chancellor to the Elector Max Joseph III. He first produced a criminal code and a code of civil procedure and then, in 1756, a civil code, the *Codex Maximilianeus Bavaricus civilis*. It was a practical law, written in clear German, with little evidence of natural law theory. It set out the Bavarian form of the *ius commune* in the familiar order of the Institutes and incidentally settled some disputed points.

The codes of Prussia and Austria were the product of much consultation. Already in 1714 King Frederick William I of Prussia, on succeeding to the throne of what were still scattered dominions, had directed the law faculty of the University of Halle, whose leading member was Christian Thomasius, to prepare within three months an intelligible

statement of private law. The project was never carried out, and
Frederick William's energies were otherwise engaged, but twenty-four
years later he commissioned Samuel von Cocceji, his minister of justice,
to prepare a new statement of the law. Unlike Thomasius, Cocceji was
a keen Romanist and tried to maintain the primacy of Roman law, but
popular feeling was against him. The public mind associated the lengthy
trials and apparently arbitrary decisions of the courts with the training
that advocates and judges had received in Roman law.

When Frederick the Great succeeded his father, he resolved to have a
code, written in German and based primarily on 'natural reason and the
character of the country', with Roman law included only if it fitted in
with them. The main draftsman was Carl Gottlieb Suarez, who shared
the view of Christian Wolff that the duty of the ruler was to lead his subjects to a perfect, rational life, in which they would be good men as well
as good citizens. The Prussian code was therefore to have an educational
function and, being addressed to the ordinary man, had to be comprehensive, clear and certain.

The final text of the *Allgemeines Landrecht*, enacted in 1794, is enormous.
It is loosely structured on Pufendorf's distinction between man as an
individual and man as a member of groups, ranging from the family,
through social classes, to the state. It comprises 19,000 articles, dealing
not just with private law but with public, criminal, feudal, ecclesiastical
and commercial laws and purports to govern much that would normally
be regarded as unsuitable for legal regulation, such as the intimate relations of husband and wife. Roman influences are noticeable mainly in
the sections on property.

In Austria, with its vast rambling provinces, each with its own separate administration and court structure, the need for unification was particularly acute. The Emperor Charles VI sponsored a unified law of
intestate succession, which was largely based on Justinian's law. This was
put into force in Upper and Lower Austria between 1727 and 1747.
Charles's successor, Maria Teresa, wanted a more comprehensive
codification. In 1753 she issued a directive to draft a code of general
private law, ignoring the laws of special groups or classes, to be based on
the *ius commune*, but using the law of reason to correct or complete it.

The first draft, the *Codex Theresianus* of 1766, was a compromise
between the traditional laws of the various provinces, with their
differing mixtures of customary and Roman elements. Its 8,367 articles
were written in the vernacular but grouped the material in Roman categories. It was attacked both by conservatives, who did not want to lose

their provincial privileges and felt that it went too far, and by reformers, who believed that it did not go far enough. The latter concentrated their fire on the Roman elements, which they said gave the code an old-fashioned look. They argued that the aim of the new code should be to get rid of obscure, mutually contradictory, laws, whether of Roman or of customary origin, and to replace them with an entirely new 'modern' law.

In the intellectual climate of the time, modern law meant natural law. The leading exponent of natural law in Austria was Karl Anton von Martini and he was clear that to jettison Roman law completely was to throw out the baby with the bath-water:

Roman civil law consists to the greatest extent of natural laws. It is possible to avoid all error if its shortcomings are complemented according to the precepts of natural law and its dark passages illuminated. Many Roman laws are arbitrary laws and some are opposed to reason. Only natural jurisprudence teaches one to distinguish arbitrary from necessary laws and improve those which are opposed to reason (*Lehrbegriff des Natur- Staats- und Völkerrechts*, Vienna 1783, para. 228)

An important feature of Roman private law was that among freemen the law made very little distinction between those of different social status. Compared with contemporary legal systems, it was less stratified. Thus, although Roman law as such was rejected, certain ideas of Roman law could be brought back under the guise of natural law.

The work of revision of the Theresian draft continued sporadically and twenty years after its publication a simpler version, reduced to a quarter of the original size, was completed and sent to provincial assemblies and the universities for their observations. The gist of their replies was that the code should give more expression to the limits which the law of reason imposed on the power of the central government. Martini produced an uneasy compromise between the view that the monarch, not being bound by the law, had the power to make whatever law he thought fit, and the view that natural law itself contained limits which no legislator could overstep.

Martini was then replaced as senior draftsman by Franz von Zeiller, who produced the code of 1,502 articles which finally came into force in 1812. Under the influence of Immanuel Kant, Zeiller accepted the distinction between morality and strict law, abandoned the notion that an agreed set of moral principles could be enacted and confined his code to what was law. He presented it as a practical compromise between Roman law, as expressing unchanging principles of reason, and the particular needs of the state. Zeiller's code has endured, with certain amendments, to the present day.

5 POTHIER AND THE FRENCH CIVIL CODE

The most famous product of the codification movement did not have the long period of gestation which characterised the Prussian and Austrian codes. The enactment of a civil code was one of the aims of the French Revolution and those who sponsored it originally had exactly opposite aims to those of Frederick the Great. They sought to sweep away the legal structure that propped up the *ancien régime*, and replace it with a short, simple code, that would express the aspirations of liberty, equality and fraternity. The Constituent Assembly had rejected two drafts when, in 1799, Napoleon seized power. He appointed a commission of four members, two from the area of the customary law and two from that of the written law, to prepare a civil code that would combine the best elements of both systems.

Fortunately the compilers of the French Code had a useful resource to hand in the works of a conspicuously unrevolutionary product of the *ancien régime*, a hereditary magistrate from Orleans named Robert Joseph Pothier (1699–1772). He had done much of the detailed preliminary work necessary for the preparation of a civil code for, as a young man, he had set himself the task of reducing both the Roman and the customary laws to a rational and usable order. He began with the problem of Justinian's Digest. He retained the original titles but rearranged all the fragments within each title in a logical order, supplying for each title an introduction and linking passages fitting the fragments together. Pothier's concern was primarily with the Roman law of antiquity but he set out the texts as illustrating rational principles of general validity. When he came to the last title on general rules, he increased the number of rules from Justinian's 211 to 960, and arranged them under five heads: general rules, rules applying to persons, things and actions, and rules of public law. The new title could serve, he thought, 'as a kind of universal index of the whole Digest'. The fruits of Pothier's labour appeared between 1748 and 1752 and gave the author international fame.

At this time he was appointed royal professor of French law in the University of Orleans and turned from Roman law, expounded in Latin, to customary law, expounded in French. In his *Coutumes d'Orléans*, published in 1761, he took up the ordering of the customary law where

Dumoulin had left it. Comparing the customs of Orleans with the other main customs, he provided in effect an introduction to French customary law in general. He then moved from the general to the particular and wrote a series of treatises on all the main parts of private law, weaving the Roman and customary elements together. The most famous was the *Traité des Obligations*, the material of which was mainly derived from Roman law. General propositions of law were always supported by illuminating illustrations, showing the operation of the rule in practice. Pothier's Obligations was quickly translated into other languages and became the model for legal treatises throughout Europe in the nineteenth century.

The Code civil, enacted in 1804, is concerned with civil law in the sense of the matters covered by the Institutional scheme but omits the topics dealt with by the Royal Ordinances. It had to be supplemented by four other codes dealing with civil procedure, criminal law, criminal procedure and commercial law. The compilers of the Code civil relied heavily on Pothier, especially in the section on Obligations, and to a lesser extent on Domat. There are, to be sure, customary elements in the French Code, such as the principle that *possession vaut titre*. But the articles stemming ultimately from Roman law predominate and they are collected in a shadowy version of the Institutional scheme. The articles are expressed in clear and succinct language, comprehensible to the ordinary man. They are collected into three books of unequal size, the first dealing with persons and the second with things, ownership and modifications of ownership. The third book, which contains over 1,500 of the 2,281 articles, is ostensibly devoted to different ways of acquiring ownership and contains all rules not appropriate for the first two books. Although amended in detail, the French Code is still in force.

6 THE GERMAN HISTORICAL SCHOOL

By the end of the eighteenth century, it must have seemed to a dispassionate observer that Roman law had ceased to be a vital force in European thought. There was, of course, a permanent sediment of Roman law terms residing in moral and political discourse and in international diplomacy. For example, in 1789 Thomas Jefferson, writing from Paris to James Madison in America, to urge the revision of the Constitution of the United States in each generation, remarked that it was self-evident that 'the earth belongs in usufruct to the living'.

Usufruct was not a term used by common lawyers, but Jefferson assumed that educated men everywhere would understand it.

The traditional function of Roman law as a source of legal ideas seemed, however, to be finished with enactment of the codes, and, even where the law was still uncodified, it was often viewed as antiquated and irrelevant. It was about this time that J. W. Goethe observed that Roman law was like a duck. Sometimes it is prominent, swimming on the surface of the water; at other times it is hidden from view, diving amid the depths. But it is always there. Just at the moment when Roman law seemed to have become no more than the subject of antiquarian study, it suddenly acquired new life.

The dramatic revival of the fortunes of Roman law in the early nineteenth century is associated with the reaction against codification and the notions of law that codification implied. The story of this revival begins with Edward Gibbon's *Decline and Fall of the Roman Empire*, of which the first volumes appeared in 1776. In the forty-fourth chapter Gibbon announced that 'the laws of a nation form the most instructive portion of its history'. He then proceeded to survey the 'revolution of almost one thousand years from the Twelve Tables to Justinian' by dividing it into three periods, each distinguished by a particular type of juristic activity. The most important was the middle (or classical) period. Gustav Hugo in Göttingen translated this chapter into German and observed that Gibbon had avoided the prevailing antiquarian approach to law in favour of Montesquieu's method, which related legal institutions to the circumstances of a particular society.

Looking at Roman law in this way demonstrated that the main agency of legal development was not legislation but debate among jurists and Hugo challenged the prevailing orthodoxy of his day by asserting that 'statutes are not the only sources of juristic truth'. The model for Hugo and his colleagues was not the law of the legislator Justinian but the law of the second century AD, when the emperor had apparently conceded to the jurists control over the development of the law through argument and debate and the giving of authoritative legal opinions. It was the jurists, therefore, who had the prime responsibility for making law.

Hugo's lead was taken up by Friedrich Karl von Savigny (1779–1861) and the German historical school which he founded. Its manifesto was the pamphlet Savigny published in 1814 entitled 'On the vocation of our age for legislation and jurisprudence'. This was written in reply to the proposal, made by A. F. J. Thibaut, to create a common civil code for all

German states, which would unify them legally in the way that the Code civil had unified the law of France.

Law was not, argued Savigny, purely a construct of reason, as the natural lawyers had presented it, but a product of the tradition and ethos of a particular society. Each nation's institutions, such as its language and its law, reflect this popular character and should change as society changes. Legislation is too blunt an instrument for legal development, which should be by custom and practice in the early stages of society and by juristic debate as society becomes more developed. Law grows 'by internal silently operating forces, not by the arbitrary will of a law-giver'. In the early period of a society, law is not sufficiently technical to be put into the form of a code; in the declining period of a society, the expertise for creating a code is lacking. The only possible period is the middle period, when there is maximum popular participation and a high level of technical expertise, expressed not by legislators but by academic jurists. But precisely because of those factors, such an age has no need of a code.

Savigny's scheme of legal development was clearly a generalisation of a view of Roman legal history which saw the law of the republic as undeveloped, regarded Justinian's law as the product of a society in decline and identified the classical period as that of maturity. Ignoring the traces of disagreement among the classical jurists, Savigny held that, far from engaging in polemics, their works show far less individuality than other types of writing; 'they all cooperate, as it were, in one and the same great work'. Their whole mode of proceeding has the certainty of mathematics. So they were able to introduce new institutions without jettisoning the old: 'a judicious mixture of the permanent and progressive principles'.

Savigny did not seek to apply his scheme of legal evolution to all societies but only to the 'nobler nations', a category which for him clearly included not only the Romans but also the Germans. There were, however, difficulties in applying his scheme of continuous historical development to German legal history in view of the break caused by the reception of Roman law. Savigny regarded this as the result of internal necessity. For Germans there was no alternative to adopting Roman law in the sixteenth century. Roman law was not a national but a supranational law, which, he declared, could no more be considered an exclusive national possession than could religion or literature.

Savigny's ideas were received enthusiastically, not only in Germany but also elsewhere in Europe, by those who for various reasons were suspicious of legislative reform and codification. The notion of the popular spirit (*Volksgeist*), enunciated by his followers, had a mystical quality, which was quite absent from Montesquieu's more rational conception of the spirit of a society's laws, but which fitted in well with the romanticism of the early nineteenth century. Some German scholars were not, however, persuaded by Savigny's justification of the reception of Roman law. Inspired by German nationalism, they considered the *gemeines Recht*, the version of the *ius commune* which still applied in most German states other than Prussia and Austria, to be a foreign law.

In the 1840s the German historical school split into two groups, Romanists and Germanists, each charged with intense emotion. For the Germanists, Roman law was an alien law and its influence was likened to a virus that had infected pure Germanic law and stunted its growth. The legal historian Heinrich Brunner referred to the influence of Roman law in the twelfth and thirteenth centuries on Bracton and Beaumanoir as 'a prophylactic inoculation', which enabled the English and French laws to escape a full reception later. The English legal historian, F. W. Maitland, sympathised with the Germanists who were researching the roots of Germanic customary law and characterised their efforts thus: 'Every scrap and fragment of old German law was to be lovingly and scientifically recovered and edited. Whatever was German was to be traced through all its fortunes to its fount. The motive force in this prolonged effort . . . was not antiquarian pedantry, nor was it a purely disinterested curiosity. If there was science, there was also love.'

The Romanists, on the other hand, led by Savigny himself, sought both to purify Roman law from its adulteration by decadent non-Roman elements and to bring out the universal principles inherent in the texts. Savigny's first task was to recover the most accurate version of the texts of Justinian and record their transition through the middle ages to his own times. He laid the foundations with his monumental *History of Roman Law in the Middle Ages*, the fruit of personal research on manuscripts in most of the main libraries of Europe. It revealed in rich detail the survival of Roman law texts in the dark ages and the revival of their study in the twelfth century. Adherents of the historical school ascribed to the intervention of Providence on its behalf a significant event that occurred just at the time when Savigny inaugurated the school. Dependence on Justinian's texts for discovering the classical Roman law was greatly reduced by Niebuhr's discovery, in the cathedral library of Verona, of an original text of Gaius's Institutes.

7 PANDECT-SCIENCE AND THE GERMAN CIVIL CODE

The German Romanists were not interested in tracing the way in which Roman law had been adapted to serve the needs of contemporary society by the work of the Commentators or the writers of the Dutch school. In a spirit of revived humanism, they wanted to reveal the inherent theoretical structure that was implicit in the texts. Savigny's model was the late-sixteenth-century humanist Hugo Donellus. In an early work on the law of possession (1803) that established his scholarly reputation, Savigny observed in the preface that Donellus was the only earlier jurist who had a clear vision of what Roman law scholarship required. Building upon certain texts which required not only physical control but also a particular intention on the part of the possessor, Savigny found the central principle of possession to be as a manifestation of the human will and re-arranged the Roman texts on possession in order to illustrate that principle.

Pandect-science, as the nineteenth-century German approach to the Roman law texts came to be called, owed more than a little to those natural law writers who saw law as a kind of legal mathematics. Savigny hoped to show that it was still possible to use the scientific concepts derived from the Pandects to solve the solution of contemporary problems.

The festering social problem for Germany in the first half of the century was the position of peasants and the need to free them from the burdensome relics of feudalism. According to the German version of the *ius commune*, peasants were considered to be *coloni*. In late Roman law *coloni* were tenants who were tied to the land in a way that foreshadowed medieval serfdom. Savigny pointed out that this conception of the colonate was the product of the period of Roman legal decline and that it should not serve as a model for nineteenth-century peasants. On the contrary, in true (classical) Roman law *coloni* had been free tenant farmers, and that version was a better model which legal science could recover.

Savigny wanted to strip Roman law of the baggage which it had accumulated for the purpose of accommodating the feudal relationship. As Donellus had demonstrated, the notion of a divided ownership, with a *dominium directum* ascribed to the lord and a *dominium utile* ascribed to the vassal, had no place in true Roman law. But if the lord and vassal did not share the *dominium*, how should their respective interests be characterised? The Roman notion of a servitude, or burden on the land, could be used to characterise both the interest of the lord and that of the vassal. For servitudes were either personal or praedial. The main personal servitude was usufruct, the right to enjoy the land for life, and it had for long been used as the model for the vassal's interest, but with the reservation that it was permanent interest. If the lord were considered as the owner, then the vassal could be regarded as a kind of permanent usufructuary of the land. Now, however, it was argued that it better fitted the current state of the feudal relationship to regard the vassal as the owner, and in that event, the lord's residual interest was more like a praedial servitude, such as a right of way over the land. The significance of this analogy was that a praedial servitude could be extinguished by prescription. If the person entitled to the right of way failed to exercise it, or if the land-owner blocked the way and the person entitled did nothing about it for a certain period, then the land was freed from the burden on it. The door was open for the idea that by prescription the vassal could similarly free himself of the feudal burdens.

The search for a purified Roman law, through which professors could find solutions to Germany's social problems without resort to reform legislation, had only limited success among judges and practitioners. They were looking for legal arguments which could justify what they wanted to do anyway, namely, free the peasants from their feudal burdens, but the historical school's agenda of reform through academic doctrinal development did not move quickly enough. The demand for reform was too pressing and it was legislation, following the revolution of 1848, which freed the peasants.

Savigny's programme of finding the central principles of Roman law, begun in the treatise on possession, was extended to the whole field of private law in his significantly entitled *System des heutigen römischen Rechts* (System of present-day Roman law), which appeared between 1840 and 1849. For Savigny there was no contradiction between his historical studies and his Pandect-science; they illustrated two sides of the same phenomenon. For his followers, however, Pandect-science became less historical and more rational. By the 1850s it was clear that, if Roman law was to have relevance in contemporary Germany, it would have to be reinvented yet again. In place of Roman law as the law that allowed maximum freedom to the human will, as Savigny's *System* portrayed it, the mood of the age required a Roman law that expressed the materialist values of a bourgeois society.

From the middle of the century it was obvious that German law was moving inexorably towards codification and that, whereas it was the professors who would prepare the code, it was the judges who would interpret it and give it effect. An all-German Commercial Code was enacted in 1861, but it was based not on Roman law but on the practice of merchants, which had inspired the French commercial ordinances of the seventeenth century. The stark fact was that Roman law, which allowed the parties great freedom to mould their transactions as they wanted, did not deal with the complex legal mechanisms of modern commercial life. The economic historian Max Weber pointed to the fact that, despite the liberal nature of Roman private law, none of the characteristic legal institutions of modern capitalism are derived from Roman law. As examples he cited annuity bonds, bearer securities, shares, bills of exchange, trading companies (in their modern capitalistic form), mortgages (as capital investment) and direct agency.

The Romanists now concentrated their efforts on preparing the substance of the civil Code. They recognised that Roman law's contribution would have to be in the form of a distillation of principles that could be incorporated into a code that would be appropriate for a commercially oriented society. To this end Roman law had to be purged of those features which recalled the non-industrial society that gave it birth and those aspects which encouraged entrepreneurs emphasised. Yet, by basing the substance of the new code on Pandect-science, the Romanists were able to claim that it was an apolitical, impartial law and that, as its exponents, they were above politics.

The two most prominent German Romanists of the second half of the nineteenth century were Rudolf von Jhering and Bernhard Windscheid, almost exact contemporaries, who both died in 1892. Jhering had a keen sense of irony and derided the stress on concepts, detached from their consequences, which characterised the prevailing Pandect-science. In his three-volume masterpiece on the spirit of Roman law (*Der Geist des römischen Rechts*), of which the first volume appeared in 1852, he wrote that

the desire for logic that turns jurisprudence into legal mathematics is an error and arises from misunderstanding law. Life does not exist for the sake of concepts but concepts for the sake of life. It is not logic that is entitled to exist but what is claimed by life, by social relations, by the sense of justice – and logical necessity or logical impossibility is immaterial. (II.2.Introd. 69)

Roman law, held Jhering, was based not on moral principles, as the natural lawyers had maintained, but on economic necessity; its guiding principle was self-promotion. Jhering did not completely reject national character as a determinant of law. The ideal character for legal growth was a balance between the conservative and the progressive forces that allowed the law to grow slowly but surely. As examples of peoples whose character had such a balance, he cited the ancient Romans and the English. Yet Jhering rejected the historical school's notion of the national spirit as a determinant of the law. The presence of Roman ideas in German law was incompatible with such a notion. The characteristic of a progressive people was precisely their ability to assimilate ideas and institutions from outside, as was shown by the Romans' incorporation of the rules of the *ius gentium* to supplement those of the *ius civile*. A progressive law, he concluded, is characterised not by nationality but by universality.

In 1857 Jhering founded a periodical for studies aimed at showing the potential of Roman law to deal with modern problems. As he announced in the first issue, its watchword would be 'through Roman law, beyond Roman law'. An important example is Jhering's own essay on the doctrine of *culpa in contrahendo*, or fault in the formation of a contract which was itself void or incomplete. He took a couple of texts in the Digest and built on them an elaborate theory according to which there could still be a contractual liability, even though there was no contract.

Windscheid made his name with a book on the action in Roman law, published in 1856. Savigny had regarded the Roman action much as Donellus had seen it, that is, actions were provided to give effect to pre-existing subjective rights, based on justice. Windscheid showed that the praetor, representing the Roman state, granted an action whenever it was state policy that a legal remedy was appropriate. The praetor did not concern himself with rights. In deciding what remedies to grant, he was guided by his sense of the economic needs of the time.

The new Pandectists did not admit that they were advocating a particular political philosophy but the legal science that they claimed to have discovered in Roman law revealed a highly individualist law. It encouraged freedom of contract without any recognition of the inequality of bargaining power. It gave the maximum protection to private property and it reduced to a minimum the liability of business men for injuries caused to others in the course of their operations. Windscheid summed up their achievement in his three-volume work on *Pandektenrecht* (1862–70), of which seven editions were published before his death in 1892. The work has been justly compared with the Great Gloss of Accursius. It synthesised the work of Pandect-science with authority and moderation and organised it in a well-arranged system that was easy to consult. Its influence on the content of the German Civil Code (BGB) of 1900 was immense.

The form of the BGB does not follow the order of the Institutes but is influenced by other earlier orders, in particular the Christian geometric systems, going back to Pufendorf and Domat, which moved from the general to the particular. First there is a General Part setting out rules common to all kinds of legal transaction and including the part of the law of persons dealing with legal capacity. Emphasis is put on the notion of *Rechtsgeschäft*, which is essentially the *negotium* of Althusius, that is, any expression of the will by which a person intends to produce a change in his legal position. Then follow four books devoted respectively to Obligations, Things, Family law and Succession. Although the order of treatment is not that of the Institutes, the categories out of which it is constructed and many of the substantive rules are recognisably Roman.

The developments just described made German legal science the dominant force in European legal thinking. True, the stock nineteenth-century ideal of a civil code, copied by nations codifying their law, was the French Code civil, the model for the Dutch, Belgian, Italian and Spanish codes. But when it came to legal science, in the sense of the interpretation of the law by jurists, German scholarship reigned supreme. Students flocked to the great German law faculties in the way they had gone to Italy in the twelfth century, France in the sixteenth century and the Netherlands in the seventeenth. This was true even of some common lawyers from England.

8 NINETEENTH-CENTURY LEGAL SCIENCE OUTSIDE GERMANY

For much of the nineteenth century, legal science in France was dominated by the 'exegetical school', which sought to make a complete break between the text of the code, as it was enacted, and the sources from which it was derived. Its members considered the words of the text to be clear and comprehensive and aimed above all for certainty in their interpretation. In the second half of the century the exegetical school came to be influenced by Pandectist ideas of general legal concepts. In Napoleon's time the Code civil had been applied to the German Rhineland and remained in force there throughout the nineteenth century. German writers wrote treatises on it, some of which were translated into French.

In the first half of the nineteenth century Italian scholars were much influenced by the French exegetical school. After the publication of the

Italian Civil Code in 1865, which immediately preceded the unification of the country, Italian scholarship took Pandect-science as its model. Works such as Windscheid's *Pandektenrecht* were translated into Italian by the leading scholars, and leading German Romanists, such as Jhering, were fêted on visits to Italy.

In England the nineteenth-century debate among those who favoured legislation as a means of reform and those opposed to it was carried on largely in terms of Roman law. This is because the subject figured prominently in the reform of English legal education in the middle of the nineteenth century. Oxford and Cambridge had kept the torch of Roman law flickering but the Inns of Court in London had ceased to be active as teaching institutions. Teaching of English law had been introduced in the ancient universities only in the eighteenth century, and produced Blackstone's encyclopedic *Commentaries on the Laws of England*, based on the Institutional scheme. It was not, however, until the nineteenth century that legal education in anything resembling the continental understanding of the term really began in England.

University College London, whose foundation owed much to the influence of Jeremy Bentham, established chairs both of English common law and of jurisprudence in the sense of legal theory. John Austin, a disciple of Bentham, was appointed to the latter chair in 1826 and immediately went to Bonn to prepare himself. Austin's general theory of law was taken from Bentham but his analysis of legal concepts came from the German Romanists. He sought systematic structure and rigorous analysis of general legal concepts and found them in such works as Savigny's treatise on possession (which he pronounced 'of all books upon law, the most consummate and masterly') and Thibaut's System of Pandect law. The contrast between such works and those of English law was striking. 'Turning from the study of the English to the study of the Roman law, you escape from the empire of chaos and darkness to a world which seems by comparison, the region of order and light.' In 1845 Nathaniel Lindley (later Lord Lindley) published a translation of the general part of Thibaut's work under the title *Introduction to the Study of Jurisprudence*.

An enthusiastic publicist for Roman law in the Pandectist sense was Henry Sumner Maine, who had been Regius Professor of Civil Law at Cambridge. In 1856 in an essay bemoaning 'the immensity of the ignorance to which we are condemned by ignorance of Roman law', he illustrated the value of a training in Roman law in providing a set of categories and instilling a particular mode of reasoning. They had permeated the discourse of moral philosophy since the seventeenth century and had dominated international law and relations. So Roman law 'is fast becoming the lingua franca of universal jurisprudence'.

In 1859 an anonymous contributor to the *Law Magazine* wrote of Roman law:

it is obvious that its definitions and classifications, its mode of thought and the internal connections of its parts are for us incomparably more important than its minuter details. The enduring merit of the Roman law is that it is the work of a people who seem to have been raised up for that particular end at a time when the vocation of races appear to have been more marked and separate than they are now. We can therefore no more dispense with the Romans to teach us law than we can with the Greeks to teach us art. (*Law Magazine* NS, 7 (1859), 382–3)

In several areas the influence of German legal science seeped into English case-law. In the eighteenth century, under the influence of such judges as Lord Mansfield, there had been a tendency to seek the general principles of jurisprudence in French works such as those of Domat and Pothier, particularly the latter's treatise on Obligations. In the nineteenth century, the general principles were sought rather in German Pandect-science.

One problem was the nature of the personality of corporations, such as joint-stock companies. In the middle of the century the most popular theory among English lawyers was that of Savigny. Only human beings had legal capacity, so that groups of people could only have legal personality by fiction. Austin introduced into English usage the term 'legal person', a translation of Savigny's *juristische Person*. According to this theory, companies were quite distinct from their members. Towards the end of the century Maitland pointed out that in Germany itself, the Fiction theory had given way to the Realist theory, based on the idea that a corporate body was an organism with a group-will, so that the law must take account of the character of those running the company. The Fiction theory was followed by the House of Lords in the case of *Salomon* ([1897] A.C.22), whereas the Realist theory found favour in the *Daimler* case ([1916] 2 A.C.307).

Another problem concerned the nature of possession and Savigny's insistence on a particular mental and physical relationship between possessor and thing possessed was frequently cited as having a general application to all developed legal systems. Likewise Savigny's view that contract law was based on the will theory and that all contracts required subjective consensus, in the sense of an actual meeting of minds, was generally accepted, even though the common law had frequently recognised a contract if the parties had behaved in such a way as to arouse reasonable expectations in each other. Pandectist ideas were taken to be notions of general jurisprudence and therefore applicable to any developed legal system.

In the second half of the nineteenth century, the Pandectist influence in England was countered by a theory, also based on Roman law, but viewed from a different perspective. In place of Savigny of the Pandects, the model was now Savigny, the founder of the historical school. The English version of the theory that legal development occurs by itself, without the need for legislation, was set out in Sir Henry Maine's treatise *Ancient Law*, whose subtitle was 'Its connection with the early history of society and its relation to modern ideas'.

Just as Savigny had based his account of legal evolution on the laws of the 'nobler nations', so Maine confined himself to 'progressive societies' (a notion he derived from the French writer Charles Comte). They turned out to be those of the Romans and the English. Roman law provided Maine with a model of a legal system that had developed over a millennium without an obvious break and he structured his account of ancient law around the development of Roman legal institutions, with occasional references to those of other Indo-European societies.

In Rome a monarchy was replaced by a republic, dominated by patricians, whose interpretation of the *ius civile* provoked the plebeians to demand the enactment of the Twelve Tables. Maine generalises the Roman experience, holding that in the earliest period of society, divinely inspired kings hand down isolated judgments, which he calls 'themistes'. Subsequently the kings lose their sacred power and are replaced by small groups of aristocrats. They have a monopoly of knowledge of the traditional customs but they abuse their power of interpretation and produce popular agitations for the recording of the customs in what Maine calls 'ancient codes'. So far the scheme is recognisably Roman but is not readily discernible in other societies and particularly has no parallels in England.

In subsequent periods of legal change, Maine was more fortunate. Certain mechanisms of legal change are found in both Roman and English law. These include the adoption of fictions to bring new situations within established categories and the introduction of equity to modify the rigidity of the traditional law, through the control of remedies by the Roman praetor and the English chancellor. Law-making by legislation as a mechanism of legal change tends to appear late.

The most influential aspect of Maine's studies of Roman law is the impetus they gave to the study of society itself. Early society, he showed, begins not with the individual but with the family group. The primitive family is dominated by the patriarch. The members are subject to the power of the paterfamilias. This form of the primitive family explains the early history of wills, property, contract and delict. Roman law, as the law of a progressive society, was distinguished by the gradual dissolution of family dependency and the growth of individual obligation in its place. 'The individual is steadily substituted for the family as the unit of which the civil laws take account . . . we seem to have steadily moved towards a phase of social order in which all these relations arise from the free agreement of individuals.' The status of the slave, the status of the female under tutelage and the status of the son in power all disappeared, to be replaced by the free agreement of individuals. Thus, concluded Maine, 'the movement of progressive societies has hitherto been a movement from Status to Contract' (ch. 5).

Austin had generalised the particular institutions of Roman law and now Maine generalised the historical evolution of those institutions. Maine himself claimed that his method was based on that of the natural sciences. At the beginning of *Ancient Law* he says that the rudimentary ideas of law in ancient societies are 'to the jurist what the primary crusts of the earth are to the geologist'. Charles Darwin's *Origin of Species* appeared at almost the same moment as Maine's *Ancient Law* and readers saw the similarity. Just as animals gradually evolve, so, it seemed, do societies. The evidence of the changes in their structure is to be found in the changes in their law. Roman law, with its unique record of unbroken change over a thousand years, evidenced throughout by written documents, was seen as the key to the discovery of the evolution of progressive societies.

Although many of his particular propositions were later controverted, and several later scholars made their name disproving them, Maine's general approach had considerable influence on the early study of anthropology and sociology. For example, in Ferdinand Tönnies' famous work *Gemeinschaft und Gesellschaft* (1887), the two contrasting types of social groups, community and society, are based on Maine's distinction between societies based on status and those based on contract. By showing the connection between ancient Roman legal institutions and the circumstances of early Roman society, Maine established the link between law and society in a manner that was fruitful for the development of the social sciences.

9 ROMAN LAW IN THE TWENTIETH CENTURY

With the coming into force of the German Civil Code in 1900, Roman law ceased to be applicable, even in a modernised form, in any significant European state. The only exception is the Republic of San Marino, which rejected the idea of a civil code and still applies the uncodified *ius commune*. In codified legal systems the Roman civil law no longer has any direct application in the courts, although in uncodified legal systems its texts are occasionally cited as exemplifying general legal principles.

Thus in an English case in 1987, involving the rights of two parties whose oil had been mixed in the hold of an oil-tanker, the judge considered certain old English cases, which suggested that where the mixing had been done wrongfully by one of the parties, the other was entitled to the whole of the mixed oil. Having decided that he was not bound by precedent to follow any of them, he stated that he was free to adopt 'the rule which justice required' and proceeded to apply the Roman rule of *confusio*. The latter would have divided the oil between the parties, according to their respective shares (which could be precisely determined), and allowed a separate claim for damages for any loss caused by wrongdoing (Inst. 2.1.27).

The virtual cessation of references to Roman law in practice had no immediate effect on its prominent position in the curriculum of European faculties of law, where it was presented as the foundation on which the institutions of modern codified civil law were based. Freed from the need to assist the development of the law in force, however, the professors of Roman law made their subject much more historical than it had been. The aim was now to reconstruct the state of classical Roman law at its peak in the second and early third centuries.

Romanists concentrated on the study of Justinian's texts rather than on the interpretations of its various commentators. Invaluable tools were provided by the German scholar Otto Lenel, who reconstructed the text of the praetor's edict and also provided a *Palingenesia iuris civilis*, which rearranged all the fragments of Justinian's Digest as far as possible in the order in which they appeared in the classical works from which they were extracted.

Textual study concentrated on the purification of those texts by the identification of interpolations, attributable either to post-classical editors or to the compilers of the Digest. The sixteenth-century humanists had begun this work, which was now taken up with renewed vigour, so that the period between the two world wars was dominated by the 'hunt for interpolations'. The textual changes were said to be indicated either formally, by the use of particular Latin expressions, which were stigmatised as Byzantine and so non-classical, or substantially, by the fact that the text seemed to state a doctrine which could be demonstrated to be unclassical. The trouble was that each of these criteria begged the question. We do not know with any certainty the kind of Latin written in the third century by, say, Ulpian, who was actually not Roman in origin but came from Tyre in the eastern Mediterranean. And we cannot know what was the classical law on most topics except through the very texts which are under investigation. In any case classical law was not a homogeneous whole but was marked by disagreements among the jurists, hints of which survived in the texts, notwithstanding the efforts of the Digest compilers to eliminate them.

The excesses of interpolation-hunting made the study of Roman law seem to many non-specialist jurists an esoteric sport quite irrelevant to modern law. As a result, the pendulum of textual criticism in the second half of the twentieth century has swung to the opposite extreme. It is now recognised that many of the signs of alteration in the Digest texts are due to the compilers' need to abbreviate them rather than to their desire to make changes of substance. In most cases, therefore, we should assume that in their present state the texts record what is substantially classical doctrine.

All the main European countries have contributed to the twentieth-century literature of Roman law, but the most intensive scholarship has been concentrated in Germany and Italy. The law faculties of the Italian universities have over a hundred chairs dedicated to the subject. When, after the collapse of communism, the countries of Eastern Europe were concerned to re-establish their credentials as participants in the tradition of Western legal culture, they revived the study of Roman law and gave it more prominence in the curricula of law faculties.

Whereas in the nineteenth century there was no sharp division between scholars of Roman law and scholars of modern civil law, the twentieth century has seen a widening gap between the two. In general, reform of the principal European civil codes has proceeded piecemeal, although two countries, Italy and the Netherlands, have introduced complete new codes, Italy in 1942 and the Netherlands in 1992 (the latter still lacks the final part). In both cases commentators have noted some softening of the terminological rigour which characterised the nineteenth-century codes.

In the middle of the century there was a movement, based in Germany, to locate the study of Roman law in the wider context of 'ancient legal history'. Attempts were made to relate Roman law to the growing information about other laws of antiquity, in particular the various Greek laws and Mesopotamian law. The study of the latter is based on the large number of tablets recording legal transactions that have been discovered by archaeologists. Such evidence is valuable as showing the law in action, but it contributes little in the way of legal argument. For none of these other legal systems of antiquity seems to have developed a class of specialist jurists, comparable to the Roman jurists. It is the fact that we have a record of the debates of the classical jurists that has given Roman law the rich texture which makes its study valuable even today.

The European movement and the institutions it has produced have resulted, during the last two decades, in a revival of interest in Justinian's law, as the law of an ancient unified Europe, and even more in the medieval *ius commune*, which transcended national boundaries and was everywhere expounded in the same way and in the same language. The institutions of European Community law are frequently described as forming the beginning of a new *ius commune*. The difference, which is sometimes overlooked, is that the medieval *ius commune* was adopted throughout Europe voluntarily, through the recognition of its superiority to any alternative, whereas the new *ius commune*, such as, for example, the rules of product liability, is imposed from above in the interest of uniformity.

Nevertheless the idea that European Community law is in some sense not a new thing but a renewal of a cultural legal unity, which once covered the whole continent, has sparked interest in what is described as 'the civilian tradition'. This study traces the development of legal doctrines from Justinian's law up to the modern codes and brings out the contributions from scholars of different countries to that development. The result of such studies has brought into relief the extent to which legal notions worked out by the Romans have usually survived, in a recognisable form, all the changes imposed on them by those seeking to adapt them for current needs.

FURTHER READING

In general, K. Zweigert and H. Kötz, *An Introduction to Comparative Law*, trans. T. Weir, Oxford 1977; H. Coing, *Europäisches Privatrecht*, II: *1800 bis 1914*, Munich 1989; A. Gambaro and R. Sacco, *Sistemi giuridici comparati*, Turin 1996.

5.1. N. Horn, 'Römisches Recht als gemeineuropäisches Recht bei Arthur Duck', in *Studien zur europäischen Rechtsgeschichte*, ed. W. Wilhelm, Frankfurt 1972, 170; K. Luig, 'The institutes of national law in the seventeenth and eighteenth centuries', *Juridical Review* (1972), 193; G. Wesener, *Einflüsse und Geltung des römisch-gemeinen Rechts in den altösterreichischen Ländern in der Neuzeit (16 bis 18 Jahrhundert)*, Vienna 1989; J. Hilaire, *Introduction historique au droit commercial*, Paris 1986.

5.2. K. Luig, 'Die Würzeln des aufgeklärten Naturrechts bei Leibniz', in *Naturrecht-Spataufklärung-Revolution*, ed. O. Dann and D. Klippel, Hamburg 1994, 61; P. Stein, 'Civil law maxims in moral philosophy', *Tulane Law Review* 48 (1974), 1075; K. Luig, 'Wissenschaft und Kodifikation des Privatrechts im Zeitalter der Aufklärung in der Sicht von Christian Thomasius', *Europäisches Rechtsdenken in Geschichte und Gegenwart: Festschrift H. Coing*, Munich 1982, 177; P. Cappellini, *Systema iuris 1: genesi del sistema e nascita della scienza delle pandette*, Milan 1984; G. Tarello, 'Sistemazione e ideologia nelle Lois civiles di Jean Domat', *Materiali per una storia della cultura giuridica*, 2 (1972), 1959.

5.4. B. Bauer and H. Schlosser, *W. X. A. Frhr. von Kreittmayr, 1705–1790*, Munich 1991; H. E. Strakosch, *State Absolutism and the rule of Law: The Struggle for the Codification of the Civil Law in Austria, 1753–1811*, Sydney 1967; A. Schwennicke, *Die Entstehung der Einleitung des Preussischen Allgemeinen Landrechts von 1794*, Frankfurt 1993; G. Dilcher, 'Die janusköpfige Kodifikation- Das preussische ALR 1794', *Zeitschrift für Europäisches Privatrecht* (1994), 446.

5.5. A. J. Arnaud, *Les origines doctrinales du code civil français*, Paris 1969.

5.6. J. P. Eckermann, *Conversations with Goethe*, trans. J. Oxenford, Everyman edn, London 1971, 313; P. Stein, *Legal Evolution: The Story of an Idea*, Cambridge 1980; J. Rückert, 'Savigny's Konzeption von Jurisprudenz und Recht, ihre Folgen und ihre Bedeutung bis heute', *TvR*, 61 (1993), 65; H. Brunner, *Grundzüge der deutschen Rechtsgeschichte*, 7th edn, Leipzig 1919, 264; F. W. Maitland, Introduction to O. Gierke, *Political Theories of the Middle Ages*, Cambridge 1900, xvi.

5.7. J. Whitman, *The Legacy of Roman Law in the German Romantic Era*, Princeton, N.J. 1990; M. John, *Politics and the Law in Late-Nineteenth-Century Germany: The Origins of the Civil Code*, Oxford 1989; F. Wieacker, *Rudolf von Jhering*, *ZSS (RA)* 86 (1969), 1; R. von Jhering, *Beiträge und Zeugnisse*, 2nd edn, edited by O. Behrends, Göttingen 1992; B. J. Choe, *Culpa in contrahendo bei R. von Jhering*, Göttingen 1988; U. Falk, *Ein Gelehrter wie Windscheid*, Frankfurt 1989.

5.8. J. Austin, *Lectures on Jurisprudence*, 5th edn., London 1885; P. Stein, 'Legal theory and the reform of legal education in mid-nineteenth-century England', in *L'Educazione Giuridica* II, ed. A. Giuliani and N. Picarda, Perugia 1979, 185 (=*Character*, 231); M. Graziadei, 'Changing images of the law in XIX-century English thought (the continental impulse)', in *The Reception of Continental Ideas in the Common Law World 1820–1920*, ed. M. Reimann, Berlin 1994; *The Victorian Achievement of Sir Henry Maine. A Centennial Reappraisal*, ed. A. Diamond, Cambridge 1991.

5.9. *Indian Oil Corp. Ltd* v. *Greenstone Shipping S.A.* [1987] 3 All E.R. 893, on which P. Stein, *Cambridge Law Journal* 46 (1987), 369; R. Knütel, 'Rechtseinheit und Römisches Recht', *Zeitschrift für Europäisches Privatrecht* (1994), 244; R. Zimmermann, *The Law of Obligations: Roman Foundations of the Civilian Tradition*, Cape Town 1990.

Index